THE UNBIASED
TRUTH

The Unbiased Truth

Using God's Word to Break Down Walls of
Division Between Churches

L. Brian Hild

Tate Publishing & *Enterprises*

TATE PUBLISHING
& *Enterprises*

The Unbiased Truth
Copyright © 2007 by L. Brian Hild. All rights reserved.

No part of this publication may be reproduced, stored in a retrieval system or transmitted in any way by any means, electronic, mechanical, photocopy, recording or otherwise without the prior permission of the author except as provided by USA copyright law.

All Scripture quotations are taken from *The New King James Version* / Thomas Nelson Publishers, Nashville: Thomas Nelson Publishers. Copyright © 1982. Used by permission. All rights reserved.

This book is designed to provide accurate and authoritative information with regard to the subject matter covered. This information is given with the understanding that neither the author nor Tate Publishing, LLC is engaged in rendering legal, professional advice. Since the details of your situation are fact dependent, you should additionally seek the services of a competent professional.

Book design copyright © 2007 by Tate Publishing, LLC. All rights reserved.
Cover design by Lindsay Behrens
Interior design by Sarah Leis

Published in the United States of America

ISBN: 978-1-5988663-1-5
07.02.05

Acknowledgements

I want to start by thanking my Lord and Savior, Jesus Christ, for using a nobody like me to do His work. We can never repay Him for the awesome sacrifice and blessings He has bestowed upon us. I thank my wife, Mindi, for digging into God's Word with me and often times giving me the objective view that I needed. Also, for her prayers, support, and patience as well as our children's: Kate, Kyleigh, Hunter, and Jacob. I thank God for my parents, who raised me to fear the Lord. I want to thank Pastors Denny and Brad for giving me many pointers. I'd like to give a special thanks to my good friend Mike, who helped me with the resources to write with. To all the countless friends and family members who have helped me with this book in some way or another, thank you, and may God bless you all.

Contents

1. Introduction to Unity 9
2. The Plan of Salvation 13
3. A New Birth through the Holy Spirit 37
4. The Effects of "Overshooting" 48
5. The Danger of Singling Out Scriptures 57
6. The Bible Formula 73
7. Putting it all Together: Part 1 Salvation and Accountability . 81
8. Putting it all Together: Part 2 The Power of the Holy Spirit . 100
9. The Conclusion 112

Introduction To Unity

So many times, Christians are asked the question, "What does your church believe?" The most popular answer seems to be: "Whatever the Bible says, that's what we believe." Certainly that's the right answer, but why, then, are there so many different denominations of the church? If everyone's reading the same Bible, then how can there be so many different interpretations of it? It is my prayer that this book can help you solve Bible doctrines by using the only infallible source that we have—the Bible itself! By letting the Bible prove our own doctrines, we can unite as believers and know for sure that we're being obedient to God's Word. I don't know about you, but when I'm judged by the Lord, I want to make sure that everything I believe is in His Word and not just something I was brought up to believe. I'm not saying you can't trust in your spiritual leaders and teachers. I thank God for them. I'm just saying that if you want to remove all human error from your beliefs for the sake of unity and your own judgment, then let the Bible do it for you.

What an awesome force the church could be if instead of disagreeing with each other over doctrines we could concentrate on destroying the enemy of this world. The sad reality is that there are many Christians in the world who want nothing to do with someone who believes in divine healing, or someone who believes you can fall from grace, or someone who sprinkles water at Baptism instead of submersing. Even though there are answers in God's Word for these beliefs, is this any reason to act as if others aren't children of God because they believe a little differently than you? In 1st Cor 1:10, Paul stresses the importance of unity in the church when he says, *"Now I plead with you, brethren by the name of our Lord Jesus Christ, that you all speak the same thing, and that there be no divisions among you, but that you be perfectly joined together in the same mind and the same judgment."* In the Bible, we see that unity in Christ has repeatedly been the key to being a powerful witness for Jesus.

I'm sure there are families today who get saved and decide they're going to start attending church. The problem comes when they're driving around looking for a church to attend, and they can't decide which one is right because of all the different denominations there are. God forbid, maybe that family just gives up and decides it's not worth the trouble. Or out of ignorance, they end up in the congregation of a cult whose beliefs will send you straight to hell.

It's important to realize the difference between different religions and different denominations. A Christian, as we'll see later, is defined by the standards that the authors set in the Holy Bible as they were inspired by the Holy Spirit to write. This group is known as the Church, or the Body of Christ. As Romans 12:5 tells us: *"so we, being many, are one body in Christ, and individually members of one another."* Any belief that does not line up with the Bible's standard for salvation is a different religion or a cult. A denomination is a division *inside* the church or the Body of Christ (Nazarene, Baptist, Lutheran, etc.). The differences that separate these Christians are not necessarily salvation issues. They are less important issues concerning everything else. However, it is still very damaging for the church to be so separated and can ultimately lead to a salvation issue if it chases someone away from the church and from God.

One of the things that God has put in my heart is to help break down these walls of division inside the church. If we try to think and act more like our Teacher, Jesus, then I think everything else will fall into place. Quite often, Jesus warned the Pharisees not to be so stuck on their traditions but to be open to the will of God. As you'll see later, I believe open-mindedness is the key to finding different truths in the Bible. That is, you may need to accept that your beliefs may not all be a hundred percent accurate just because it's what you've been brought up to know.

I learned a long time ago that there are many different ways that people interpret the same scriptures, but there is only one *Truth*! There's only one way that God intended the Bible to be interpreted—His way. Sure, there are some mysteries that we will have to wait to get to heaven to figure out. But it would be a copout to say that every doctrine that requires a little work to accurately find fits in that category of "unsolvable mystery."

As you go through each chapter, you will see what to do and what not to do to get a better understanding of the Bible. Please understand that in no way do I believe everything in this book must be correct. I'm just as human as the next person. Even though God revealed so many things to me in this book, there is always a chance to have human error in the translation as well as in the revelation. The Holy Bible is the only *guaranteed* accurate Word of God. The purpose here is to eliminate as much of that human error as possible. Everything in this book has been the subject of years of studying, prayer, and fasting. Nothing in this book has been thrown in on a whim for flashy reading. The title, *The Unbiased Truth*, is not meant to be a dogmatic theme of "this is the only way it can be!" "Unbiased" here only means that I am trying to write this book without any denominational influence. Certainly my beliefs may not agree with everyone's, but it's my prayer that by reading this book, you will dig into Bible mysteries and doctrines like never before. I hope God will reveal many truths to you as He did to me.

It's not always enough to believe in something just because you were taught that way. Your beliefs will be so much more effective if you know exactly *why* you believe them. For example, if I told you I had a twenty-dollar bill in my pocket, you would probably believe me as a man of God. But if I pulled that bill out of my pocket and showed you, now you have infallible proof that what I said was true, and you can have all the faith in the world in that.

We as believers in Christ have a source that has proven to be just as infallible as seeing with your own eyes—the Holy Bible, the sixty-six books of God's revealed Word for us to use as an instruction manual on how to have a relationship with Him. When you can find the solutions to certain Bible doctrines by searching *all* of the scriptures that are related to that subject, then you can be sure of that doctrine and have more faith in it. This is because you've seen it with your own eyes by using the Book that God gave us. I know in my heart that every word in the Bible is accurate and was inspired by the Holy Spirit for a reason. This divine inspiration only applies to the thirty-nine Old Testament books and the twenty-seven New Testament books. Anything else that has ever been written can be used as a guide but not as an infallible source like the Bible. It would be illogical to think that the Bible had some books or even verses missing when we serve such a powerful God. If God could create the world and everything in it in only six days, then I think He's quite capable of preserving His entire Word for His children to have as an instructional manual for direction. Anyone who has studied the Bible in great detail will tell you that no human being could have ever come up with all of the fulfilled predictions and the wisdom that the Bible contains. There had to have been a divine power behind the authors. We are told in 2nd Timothy 3:16 what the inspired power was: *"All Scripture is given by inspiration of God, and is profitable for doctrine, for reproof, for correction, for instruction and righteousness..."* The Word of God is also what defines us as disciples of Jesus and sets us free. Jesus tells us in John 8:31–32, *"...If you abide in My word, you are My disciples indeed. And you shall know the truth, and the truth shall make you free."* So since we're going to be judged by the Bible, then shouldn't we live our lives according to it?

I have written this book both for the non-Christians and for the believers so that it may profit all the readers alike. For the educated readers who are advanced in Bible wisdom, some of the basic teachings will be a review. For those of you who are fairly new to God's Word, I'll try to explain everything accordingly. All of the Bible references listed in this book are taken from the Nelson translation in the New King James Version. Some bold type has been added for emphasis.

The Plan Of Salvation 2

Before I get into how to interpret the Bible better, I think it's important that we get a better understanding of what has become our basis for Christianity—God's plan of salvation. God says in Hosea 4:6, *"My people are destroyed for lack of knowledge . . ."* so I think that it's important to explain this plan by using the Bible as our reference. It appears as though there has been a generational gap in which the very basis of Christianity has been taken for granted. I think that many pastors, Sunday School teachers, and parents have just assumed that everyone knows the reason why we believe the way we do. However, as time goes on, it is more and more obvious that many people in the world don't know the reason for our Christian faith. This is a strong angle that the devil can use to twist the truth and badly deceive the uneducated ones.

Understanding God's plan for his children is the center from which other Bible doctrines will fall into place. I hope that most of us, at least, can agree on this very heritage of our Christian faith. As you read this chapter, please use the Scripture references that are provided to support any disagreements or questions that you may have. I follow a strict rule in my Christian walk. That is, no matter what I was taught or no matter what I believed before, what the Bible says takes precedence over everything. That means if there was a particular doctrine that I was raised to believe and then I learned later that it didn't line up with the Bible, I would change my belief. *Too often, people try to twist the Bible to line up with their beliefs. What we need to do is to twist our beliefs to line up with the Bible!* That can sometimes be hard to do, but if we all agree on that one principle, then we can understand the Word better and unite instead of argue.

I. Free Will

First of all, it's important to understand that we were created for God's pleasure and that it was pleasing for Him to give us all our own free will. Let's look at that for a minute. How exciting would it be if God "programmed" us to do exactly what He wanted every second of the day? There may never be any disappointments this way, but there would never be any pleasant surprises, either. Psalms 139 tells us that God has the ability to know anything He wants to about us; He's omniscient. I also believe that He has the ability to sit back and watch certain things play out for themselves without choosing to "foresee" the outcome if that's His desire.

In the Bible, we see that God would choose to reveal the beginning (Genesis) and the end (Revelation), yet He would let us fill in some of the middle before He decided what He was going to do next. Let's look at some occasions in the Bible where God waited to see an event come to pass before He acted.

King Hezekiah was told to get his house in order because he was soon going to die. After the king prayed for more time, God changed His mind and gave Hezekiah fifteen more years (Isaiah 38:1–4). When God tested Abraham with the sacrifice of his son Isaac and saw that Abraham really was going to go through with it, the Lord stopped, *"And He said, Do not lay your hand on the lad, or do anything to him; for **now** I know you fear God"* (Gen 22:12). Just before He flooded the earth, God was *"... **sorry** that He had made man on the earth, and He was grieved in His heart"* (Gen 6:6). That doesn't mean that God made a mistake, it just means that man's own free will screwed up what could have been an incorruptible world. When God anointed Saul as the king over Israel, He later regretted that decision because of Saul's disobedience. In 1st Sam 15:11, God told Samuel, *"I greatly regret that I have set up Saul as king, for he has turned back from following Me, and has not performed My commandments..."* God could have used foresight for this event and chose not to make Saul the king, but He allowed Saul the free will to rule over His people, and Saul let Him down by not following directions. I know that everything God has ever done has been perfect and that any changes in God's original plan came from our sins. Knowing this, it would be impossible for God, who is perfect, to be sorry about a decision He made unless He chose not to foreknow the outcome of that event. Jeremiah 31:34 tells us that under the new covenant, God will not remember our sins anymore. This doesn't mean that He can't remember them. It just means that He chooses not to. So here's proof that God has the ability to turn off the knowledge if He wants to. If you believe that God doesn't choose to foresee certain events, then all of these Bible examples would have to be mistakes. Our prayers must also affect God's actions; otherwise, why would He want us to pray?

When I first began to study whether or not God always uses foresight, it really took me out of my comfort zone because I never heard anyone ever suggest it before. The last thing I would ever want to do is to belittle or blaspheme God. However, I know it's not blasphemy or false teaching to believe something as long as the whole Bible backs it up. It's important to know who God truly is according to His Word. One thing that some Christians like to do is add phrases to God's Word like, "It wasn't really wine; it was grape juice," or "Jesus didn't actually let a harlot wash His feet." God doesn't need us to add anything to the Bible to make Him or His Son seem greater or holier. He does that on His own. God gave us His living Word not to change it, but to read it, understand it, and obey it in order to know Him better. God has the ability and the right to know or choose not to know anything He wants. If you think that it's impossible for God not to foresee some things, then it seems like you might be putting limitations on His ability. God can do or choose not do anything He wants. Which statement would be worse: "God may choose not to foresee every choice that we'll ever make," or "God must foresee everything, because He doesn't have the ability to do otherwise"? I wouldn't limit God to anything.

You might ask, "Why wouldn't He want to foresee everything?" In order to answer this question, you have to remember that we were created for His pleasure. Let me give you some examples in our own terms to explain this. Your friend tells you to watch a particular movie because it's the best movie he or she has ever seen. Would it be more pleasing for you to know how it ends before you watch it, or would you rather see how it plays out yourself? How much fun would it be to watch a sporting event when you already knew the final score? Would it be pleasing if you had a golf club that could hit a hole-in-one every time you swung it, and you knew that every time you played eighteen holes of golf your score would be eighteen? Yeah, maybe at first that might be fun, but after a while that would get pretty boring, wouldn't it? Here's another example. Would you rather be married to someone who loved you for who you are, or would it be better for your spouse to just settle for you because he or she was forced to? God has pleasure when we choose Him by our own accord. Yes, it hurts Him when we make bad choices with our free will, but when we choose to serve Him and love Him, not because we're forced to, but because we want to, then God gets the pleasure He created us for.

II. The Fall of Lucifer and The Fall of Man

To understand God's whole plan, we have to go all the way back to the time when there was a mighty angel in Heaven named Lucifer. He had charge over many of God's angels. In Ezekiel 28, God describes Lucifer (who He refers to here as the King of Tyre) as a *"...seal of perfection. Full of wisdom and perfect in beauty."* (Ez. 28:11). The Lord continues to describe him in Ezekiel 28:13–15 as an *"... anointed cherub ..."* covered in precious stones. In verse 15, God tells Lucifer, *"You were perfect in your ways from the day you were created..."* At one point, Lucifer's pride grew overwhelmingly, and he thought he was going to exalt himself above almighty God. The sin of Lucifer and his angels caused God to cast them out of Heaven. Isaiah 14:12–14 tells it like this:

> "How you are fallen from heaven, O Lucifer, son of the morning! How you are cut down to the ground, you who weakened the nations! For you have said in your heart: 'I will ascend into heaven, I will exalt my throne above the stars of God...I will be like the Most High.'"

Sometime after Lucifer fell, sin came into the world because of Adam and Eve's disobedience.

Let's go to the Garden of Eden and look at where it started. God formed the first man, Adam, out of the dust of the earth and breathed life into him (Gen. 2:7). God didn't want to force Adam to obey Him, so He gave him one tiny little command and one huge consequence if he broke it. God told Adam that he could eat from any tree in the Garden except the tree of knowledge of good and evil. God added that if Adam disobeyed Him, he would surely die (Gen. 2:16–17). By giving this command, God gave Adam free will, like I just discussed earlier. Since God allowed Adam the free will to choose either good or evil, this kind of opened a door for Lucifer. Because of the fact that God is pure holiness, Lucifer, who came in the form of a serpent, had an opportunity to step in as the evil side of free will to tempt Adam. James 1:13 tells us that God doesn't tempt anyone. We also know that Satan tempted Jesus in the wilderness (Mark 1:13). The one conclusion we can draw here is that whenever God gives us free will, He will allow Satan to tempt us. Given this, Lucifer regained some authority after being cast out of Heaven and was allowed to tempt Adam and Eve. Since you and I have free will today, Satan is able to tempt us just the same.

There are probably no words to describe the terrible feeling that rushed throughout the earth on that sinful day when Adam and Eve disobeyed God's only commandment. Imagine, all of the sudden, a new side of God's creation. The animals begin fighting each other, trees and plants start dying, there was pain and suffering, and for the first time, death. But the worst hurt of all was when God realized that sin came in and defiled His creation of mankind. At that point, God knew He had to separate Himself from the sin of mankind, so He ordered Adam and Eve to leave the beautiful Garden of Eden. One thing you have to realize is that God the Father is much too holy and pure to remain in the presence of sin. None of us can understand that level of holiness that God is. For that reason, the separation between our holy Lord and sinful man was necessary.

Now because of sin, we can see in greater detail how Lucifer (Satan) regained some of that authority that he had before he was cast out of Heaven. Before sin came into the world through Adam and Eve (known as The Fall), God would come down in the cool of the evening and walk with them. Without the physical presence of God that was once with Adam and Eve, Satan became the ruler over the physical world (John 12:31). Satan was also able to gain the power over death, because death was the consequence of their sin (Heb. 2:14). This may seem like a harsh consequence to Adam, especially since we have this one grave mistake to thank for all the death, sickness, famine, and all other wickedness of the world today, but remember that God did warn Adam beforehand what would happen if he disobeyed. God honored His Word just like He always has and always will. He gave them free will, and they chose to disobey Him. God didn't want them to fall into sin and bring death into the world. It's God's will that none should perish (2nd Pet. 3:9). But He didn't want to control Adam and Eve's actions, either.

Indeed, God was very disappointed in Adam and Eve, but He still loved them and the rest of His creation so much that He came up with a plan to save all of His creation. You see, God is a righteous Judge who must execute His judgment fairly and justly. Otherwise, anarchy would be the way of life for us all. Moses describes this side of God in Deuteronomy 32:4. Here he states, *"He is the Rock, His work is perfect; For all His ways are justice, A God of truth and without injustice; Righteous and upright is He."*

Since Adam and Eve deliberately disobeyed God (as we all have) and caused sin to come into the world, God had to give punishment accordingly. We know from Romans 6:23 and Isaiah 59:1–2 that the punishment was eternal death and total separation from our Creator. The price for this sin was more than we as mere humans could ever pay. There was nothing Adam and Eve or any one of us could ever do to restore the sin barrier between man and God. God could have easily just scrapped out the world and started over. In fact, He would have been just and fair in doing that. However, in John 3:16, Jesus tells us about the awesome plan God had when He says, *"For God so loved the world that He gave His only begotten Son, that whoever believes in Him should not perish but have everlasting life."* So God didn't give up on mankind. He provided a plan to save us. For God the Father, the most upsetting part of His plan was that the only sacrifice that would ever be sufficient enough to break down that wall of sin between Him and mankind was the death of His only begotten Son. Nonetheless, God did make the choice to send His Son to die for us. Jesus offered to give His own life for the punishment that we all deserved.

Right after The Fall of Man in the garden, God addressed this situation. The Bible is not clear here as to how God was manifested when He addressed Satan. He may have been revealed through His Son Jesus or through the Holy Spirit as He faced Satan (possibly the same in Job 1). Whichever way, we know the Bible says God told Satan that for his punishment, "Eve's Seed" was going to bruise his head (Gen. 3:15). God didn't tell the devil when this person was coming or how he was going to defeat him. Satan may not have even know that it would be God's Son who would fill this role. God just warned him that it was going to happen. This promised descendant of Eve was Jesus, also called the Messiah or the Christ. As the Bible tells us, it wasn't until thousands of years later that this promise was fulfilled. There are two main reasons for this long wait. For one, God's time schedule is a lot different than ours. 2nd Peter 3:8 tells us that, "... *with the Lord one day is as a thousand years, and a thousand years as one day.*" We tend to think in terms of days or years, but God thinks in terms of eternity. The second reason for the long delay, I believe, is because God dreaded so badly what He was going to have to watch His Son go through in order to completely free us from the bondage of the original sin of Adam.

You see, when Adam disobeyed God, it caused a "sin virus" in the human body that would be passed on through every generation after that. This original sin is passed down not through the mother, but through the father. Originally, Adam was created for God, and Eve was created for Adam. Adam was the one who God gave the command to before Eve was even created. Therefore, it was Adam's disobedience, not Eve's, that was responsible for the fall of man and for that virus of sin to be spread from then on. For this reason, men and women alike are all born into a sinful body, but it's only passed on through the father. We'll look at why this is important later.

III. Satan's Plan To Stop The Messiah

Hundreds and hundreds of years went by following The Fall of Man. Satan obviously didn't want this promised "Seed of Eve" to come and destroy him, so Genesis 6 tells us about an evil plan to try to stop Him from coming. There have been many different beliefs as to what this part of Scripture was referring to. The following explanation is just one view of a massive satanic plan. There's not a lot of Scripture base, so some speculation may be required. I believe it is a relevant part of knowing God's entire plan as this sets the stage for the great flood.

Genesis 6:2 tells us that, *"sons of God saw the daughters of men, that they were beautiful; and they took wives for themselves of all whom they chose."* As we read later, these wicked "sons of God" would impregnate the human women, and they would bore wicked offspring called "giants." Genesis 6:4 goes on to say, *"There were giants on the earth in those days, and also afterward, when the sons of God came into the daughters of men and they bore children to them . . . "* Since the offspring between the "sons of God" and the human women were evil, then that makes a strong case for these "sons of God" being those evil angels that were once cast out of Heaven with Lucifer. Another reason why I believe these "sons of God" that are spoken of were once God's heavenly angels that were cast out with Lucifer is because we see them used in conjunction in Job 1. In the sixth verse of Job 1, the "sons of God" together with Satan apparently tried to turn Job from the Lord. So these sons of God could easily be the evil angels that were cast out of Heaven. If this is the case, then the devil sent these foul angelic beings to infect all of the women with this evil satanic gene pool. The fathers already passed down original sin to their children, but the mothers would now be affected with this evil by giving birth to pure wickedness. Satan must have known a little bit of how God operated, having been in such a high position in Heaven. Surely no Redeemer of God could ever have been born if Satan could infect all of the women with this kind of evil. If this plan would have worked, then both the mother's seed and the father's seed would have been destroyed. This would disable any pure Godly offspring from coming.

Over time, God looked at how His creation was completely destroying itself from this evil. Genesis 6:5 says, *"Then the Lord saw that the wickedness of man was great in the earth, and that **every** intent of the thoughts of his heart was **only evil** continually."* Apparently, when this satanic gene pool infected people, their soul would be defiled just like their physical bodies from the original sin of Adam. Again, this would disable any righteous seed of Eve from destroying Satan. Verses six and seven go on to say that God was grieved in His heart and that He was sorry He ever made man. This again proves that we can actually disappoint God as He waits sometimes to see the choices that we make. Otherwise, why would a perfect God deliberately do something that He was later going to be sorry for unless He chose not to foresee the event beforehand?

IV. The Flood

This string of "satanic DNA," which is not to be confused with original sin of Adam, apparently reached every man, woman, and child on the earth, except one man's family. Genesis 6:12 tells us that, *"…**all** flesh had corrupted their way on the earth."* That is, all except one man and his family. Genesis 6:8–9 tells us, *"But Noah found grace in the eyes of the Lord…Noah was a just man, perfect in his generations. Noah walked with God."* Noah being "perfect in his generations" didn't mean that he was a perfect person; only Christ could claim that. It means that his genealogy or his generations were perfect, all the way back to Adam and Eve. This statement means that Noah and his seven family members hadn't been tainted by that wicked gene of the giants. These eight people (Noah and his wife and their three sons and wives) were still born into that original sin from Adam, but they were not the offspring of those evil angels. Not only was Noah's family lineage still pure all the way back to Adam and Eve, but they were obedient to God as well. So naturally, God found favor with Noah and with his family. He instructed Noah to build an ark so He could escape the great flood that was going to come and remove all of this evil. When God flooded the earth, it killed all of the devil-infested giants, and it sent the spirits of those wicked angels that were on the earth into hell to be locked up. 2nd Peter 2:4–5 tells us that,

> "... God did not spare the angels who sinned, but cast them down to hell and delivered them into chains of darkness, to be reserved for judgment; and did not spare the ancient world, but saved Noah, one of eight people... bringing in the flood on the world of the ungodly."

This great flood of the world, as destructive as it was, wasn't done out of hatred or even punishment. It was done because the mercy and love that God has for us is so great that He wasn't going to let anything stop His plan to save us all. Again, He could have just wiped out the entire earth and started over if He wanted to, but God honors His own Word so much that He never goes back on it. If God hadn't put a stop to that wickedness, the Messiah wouldn't have come to redeem us. We wouldn't have even been born if Satan was successful because humanity was on pace to destroy itself. Not to mention that the righteous people who already died would have never had the opportunity to be with God. In short, God loved us so much that He sent rain on Satan's plan in order to fulfill His original plan.

V. After-life For The Righteous

If we move ahead in time between The Fall of Man and when Christ died on the cross, then we can see in more detail the morbid consequence of sin. So what happens during this B.C. period of time when someone died? To answer this, you have to realize that every person who was ever born has a soul, and that soul will live forever no matter what. The good news is that we control whether the eternal life of our soul will be indescribably pleasant or non-stop torture forever. This place of torment is for all of the wicked people who have abused their free will and have opposed God. The Bible calls this place hell (Psalms 55:15). Mark 9:43–44 gives us a disturbing image of this place when Jesus says hell is a place *"where 'Their worm* (the soul of the unrighteous people) *does not die, And the fire is not quenched."*

There was also a place of waiting before Jesus came where there was comfort for all of the righteous and godly people. This place was called Paradise (Luke 23:43). It was also referred to as Abraham's Bosom (Luke 16:22). This afterlife waiting place was reserved for the souls of those godly people who died. Paradise is not to be confused with Heaven. Heaven is the abode of Almighty God and His holy angels. Even after death, the souls of righteous men and women had not been redeemed of their sins yet so that they could be in the presence of God in Heaven. Not to mention, Satan had the power over death (Heb. 2:14), which is why Abraham's Bosom and hell were very close to each other, separated only by a great gulf. In fact, Luke 16:19-31 tells us that the two places were so close that the rich man in hell could cry out to Abraham. Although this Paradise was an underworld holding cell, God still comforted them there and kept them from evil until they could be permanently freed of their sins and reunited with Him.

God gave laws and covenants to His people so that the ones who were obedient could have at least some type of relationship with Him. Before Christ died, forgiveness of sins was only a temporary covering up by way of animal sacrifices and atonement from the High Priest. It wasn't a complete removal or washing away of their sins. Hebrews 10:1 confirms this by telling us that these same sacrifices that are offered year by year can never "... *make those who approach perfect.*" This is why the righteous ones who died could not go to Heaven yet to be with God. Before Christ came and died as a final sacrifice for our sins, there was nothing that the people could do to sufficiently remove the sins that they committed. Nor could they remove the original sin that they were born into. Since covering up sins required atonement from the High Priest, animal sacrifices, certain offerings, and other rituals, then you can see how this was an incomplete and a temporary covenant that God had with His people. That is what Jesus meant when He said, *"Do not think that I came to destroy the Law. I did not come to destroy but to fulfill"* (Matt. 5:17). He completed or fulfilled an incomplete plan of salvation through His death and resurrection. By Him doing that, it made the old Law of Moses obsolete (Heb. 8:13).

As a child, I used to wonder why I was raised to be a Christian and not a Jew, since Jesus was a Jew. Now I realize that the repetition of Jewish Law is something that Jesus freed us from. Romans 7:4 tells us, *"Therefore, my brethren, you also have become dead to the law through the body of Christ..."* Again in Romans 7:6, it says, *"But now we have been delivered from the law..."* Sometimes Christians will add some of these Old Testament laws and rituals to their New Testament beliefs. When we add anything extra to what Jesus already finished, it's kind of like saying that His death wasn't good enough. The Law still serves the purpose of teaching us right from wrong, especially from a moral standpoint. Paul tells us in Romans 7:7 that, *"...I would not have known sin except through the law..."* However, it no longer makes one righteous like it used to (this will be explained in greater detail in Chapter 7, Accountability). In order to be found righteous through the Law, you needed to do certain works. Now we're saved through our faith in Christ, which is evident through our good works and deeds.

VI. How To Join Sinful Man Back With A Holy God

For now, let's continue with the Old Testament saints. In order for these righteous people to be reunited with the God again, two things had to happen. First, physical death was required because their bodies were corrupt with the original sin of Adam. These sinful bodies, in part, kept them from inheriting Heaven. 1st Corinthians 15:50 tells us that, *"...flesh and blood cannot inherit the kingdom of God..."* This is another reason why Adam had to leave the Garden of Eden. The Tree of Life was inside that Garden (Gen. 2:9), and as long as Adam ate the leaves of it, he wouldn't die. Revelation 22:2 tells us that this tree was *"...for the healing of the nations."* God needed Adam's physical body to die, not to be healed, in order to be rejoined with Him.

The same necessity of bodily death applied to everyone after him. However, there were two exceptions to this rule in the Old Testament. Enoch (Gen. 5:24, Heb. 11:5) and Elijah (2nd Kings 2:11) were taken to Heaven, not Paradise, without ever dying. God's reasoning here was probably to serve a later purpose in the great tribulation period when these two men will likely return to the earth as the "two witnesses" mentioned in Revelation 11. We must assume that

God personally purified them before they entered Heaven since they were born into sin like everyone else. Perhaps they were changed, "... *in the twinkling of an eye,*" like the raptured saints will be (1 Cor. 15:51–52). Whatever the case may be, we know that the Bible says our earthly bodies cannot inherit the kingdom of God, so they must have been changed into some type of body pure enough to be in the presence of God. Aside from these two exceptions (and the raptured saints), death of the sinful body is necessary to be joined with God. 1st Corinthians 15:35–49 describes how our natural body must die so our spiritual body can be made alive.

The second thing that was required for all of God's people to be rejoined with Him was this: They needed a High Priest who could offer a sacrifice that was not only sufficient enough to absorb the sins of the past, but all of the sins of the future as well. They needed a sacrifice that could take on the punishment for every sin that ever has been or ever will be committed. They needed one that could pay the penalty for every person in history. This sacrifice would have to be absolutely perfect and without any flaw at all so that it would *never* have to be repeated again. This one who would later redeem us of our sins could not have been born into a body that carries the original sin of Adam. That wouldn't have been acceptable enough to take the place of all sins, because then he would need somebody to redeem himself. Since all men and women are born into sin, this condition rules out every human being on the earth. The truth is there was nothing on the earth that was sufficient enough to take the place of all the sin from the beginning of man to the end. God the Father, of course, already knew what it would take to properly redeem mankind. Back in Genesis, God told the devil that "Eve's seed" would destroy him. Any other man in the Bible would have been referred to paternally as "Adam's seed." All throughout the Bible, family lineage was recorded through the fathers' side. By God telling the devil that, "her seed shall bruise your head" and not "his seed," then we can see how this sets the stage for a virgin birth. That is, a physical birth without a human father.

VII. The Virgin Birth

The only way to be physically born without a father would be for God to personally perform a divine miracle. Since the omnipresent power of God is the Holy Ghost, then this infant would have to be conceived "of the Holy Ghost" (Luke 1:35). If a man could come into the world by being born of the Holy Spirit and a human woman, then he could avoid being born into that original sin. As I said before, we are all born into original sin, but it is only passed down through the human father because of the accountability of Adam. If original sin was passed down through the mother as well as the father, then we would have to assume Christ was born in sin just like the rest of us from His mother Mary. He Himself would need to be redeemed from sin just like us. This shows us that original sin only is passed down through the father. If you remove the human father and replace him with the Holy Ghost, then you've got a sinless child. In order for this sacrifice to be good enough to save humanity, He Himself would have to be totally human and would have to be tempted like everyone else (Heb. 2:18). If this same child grew up and carried out the will of God with absolute perfection and without ever sinning, then the plan of salvation would be completed. Nothing short of this awesome sacrifice would be sufficient enough to completely remove sin from the world.

As it turns out, there was only one person who could ever come to the earth completely free of original sin. There was only one man who was holy and perfect enough to carry out this impossible task without falling into temptation. That man was none other than Jesus Christ, the Son of the Living God.

Jesus, who was also referred to as the Word of God made flesh (John 1:14), was the Creator of the Heavens and earth from the beginning. There was nothing ever made that was not made through Him (John 1:1–3). He is one third of an incredible force that we call the Godhead (1st John 5:7, Col. 2:9). God the Father gives the plan or the will. The Son of God designs and perfects the plan as an architect would. The Holy Spirit is the agent or the power through which the plan is fulfilled. The Bible shows us that God always works in this manner. Even salvation requires all three people of the

Trinity in order for it to happen. To have eternal life with the Father, we must believe in His Son, Jesus. When we do this, then we receive the Holy Spirit.

Imagine what it must have been like for Jesus to be the Creator of all things, the Son of God, the Messiah, and the beginning and the end. Imagine having the fullness of the Godhead at your disposal (Col. 2:9) and sitting in glory at the right hand of God the Father (Ps. 110:1). Now, if you can, picture this. Jesus loved us so much, and He honored His Father's will so much, that He voluntarily left His glorious place in Heaven. He came to earth and spent at least 33 years away from His divine position in Heaven just so He could be beaten and brutally killed for something that we did. Don't we serve an awesome God? I can almost feel the hurt when unsaved Jews and other non-believers refuse to accept Jesus as the only Way to salvation after all that He went through for us. I know that He feels the most hurt, though.

VIII. Why Satan Never Saw It Coming

Let's look at the strategy that God used that was so shocking to everyone, especially Satan, who never saw this coming. You see, the devil probably knows the Word of God better than we do. He even quoted from it when he tempted Jesus in the wilderness (Matt. 4:6). Since sinful man had to share the earth with Satan as the ruler of it (John 12:31, John 14:30), then that gave the devil the same access to God's Word as man had (at least the material part of God's Word such as manuscripts, scrolls, etc.). Knowing this, God was careful not to let the devil figure out exactly how His Son was going to defeat him. If the older books of the Bible would have came out and said word for word what His strategy was before Jesus came, then Satan and his angels could have had a better chance of stopping it. This is exactly the reason why we need the Holy Spirit to teach us the mysteries of God (John 14:26). When we live our life in the spiritual realm and not in the worldly realm, Satan can not interfere with us. With the Holy Spirit inside of us, we can figure out mysteries that the devil cannot. It is this very same reason why unbelievers can't understand the Bible. You need the Holy Spirit's guidance.

In God's Word, He gave the righteous people from the Old Testament days more than enough hope of one day having eternal life with Him. But God didn't give too much information away so that Satan could be expecting it. Satan thought that *by* Jesus' death, it would end any attempt to defeat him. He didn't know that victory would come *because* of Jesus' death. In Romans 16:25–26, Paul tells us that the revealing of Jesus Christ was a prophetic mystery that had been kept a secret since the world began, but now He was made known to all nations. You see, the devil is very sneaky and witty, but he is no match for our omniscient God. That's why we have to believe in the Bible *by faith*. We can't always reason everything out because His ways are so far above our ways, and we can't always understand why He does everything the way He does. We can, however, be at peace knowing that God has everything in place for a specific reason. We may not always know the reason, but that's where our faith comes in. That's where we need the Holy Spirit to guide us.

So now, in hindsight, let's look back at Jesus' life and death so we can begin to see how He defeated Satan and took back the power over death. Jesus was not born into a sinful body, nor did He ever sin while He was on the earth. This enabled Jesus to have an exceptionally close relationship with His Father because there was no wall of sin separating the Two. We can have this same relationship by being "born again" and by repenting (as I will discuss in Chapter 3). Jesus constantly stayed in prayer and fasted so that everywhere He went, He could heal people of their sicknesses or anything else the "evil one" put in His way. However, the greatest gift of all that He offered was the promise of eternal life, or salvation. Finally, after thousands of years, Jesus came and offered a way for us to be free from the bondage of the devil.

Before Jesus could free those captives that were held in Paradise, He had to face Satan in person. He had to take back the power over death that was holding the righteous saints in bondage. This means that Jesus would have to die and then descend into the lowest parts of the earth where He could confront the devil. Matthew 12:40 tells us that, *"For as Jonah was three days and three nights in the belly of the great fish, so will the Son of Man be three days and three nights in the heart of the earth."* Again in Ephesians 4:8–9, Paul tells us *"... When He ascended on high, He led captivity captive... Now this, "He ascended"—what does it mean but that He also first **descended** into the lower parts of the earth?"* The big question is, "How did the holiest Man ever to walk the face of the earth get into such an unholy place, since we already know that God is too holy to be in the presence of sin?" The answer to this question will give us all a much greater appreciation for who Jesus Christ really is.

IX. He Became Sin So We Might Be Sinless

If we go to the cross a couple thousand years ago, there we'll find the suffering that Jesus really had to go through. I'm not talking about the brutal beating that He took. I'm referring to the inner hurt that none of us could ever bear or even imagine. It's important to know that many times when there was a sacrifice for sin, the object of that sacrifice had to take the place of the sin or "absorb" the sin. Before Jesus, these objects of sacrifice were certain animals followed by various rituals. On one day a year, the Day of Atonement, the High Priest would find a pure, spotless goat. The High Priest would then lay his hands on the goat and begin to confess the sins of all God's people. As he confessed these sins and asked for God's forgiveness, the sin was then absorbed into the goat (Lev. 16:21–22). Once the Priest was done, they took the goat deep into the wilderness and let it go. This was a symbol of sin being separated from man.

As Jesus was dying on the cross, He, too, confessed the sins of the people and asked for His Father for our forgiveness (Luke 23:24). The difference was that instead of Jesus being the High Priest of that time, He would be the last High Priest for anyone who accepted Him. Instead of an animal sacrifice that would have to be repeated over and over, He perfected one sacrifice that would never have to be repeated. Instead of just one year's worth of the Jewish people's sins, Jesus took all of the sin for *all* people from Adam on. Every sin that was ever committed and every sin that ever will be committed was absorbed into Jesus' body that day. Isaiah 53:6 says, *"...the Lord has laid **on** Him the iniquity of us all."* Isaiah 53:11 says, *"...He shall **bear** their iniquities."* 2nd Corinthians 5:21 confirms this by stating that

God made Jesus "...*who knew no sin* **to be sin** *for us, that we might become the righteousness of God in Him.*"

While Jesus was nearing the end of His physical life, He cried out something that really defines who He is. He said in Luke 23:34, "...*Father, Forgive them, for they know not what they do...*" I can't imagine asking God to forgive someone while they were in the middle of killing me, but Christ is more merciful than we could ever comprehend. Nonetheless, there has never been a more important statement than this. The will of the Father was nearing the end on earth. The sacrifice was almost completed. Now the final High Priest was confessing and asking His Father to forgive all the sins of the past, present, and future. He willingly took on all of that sin into Himself, just like the sacrificial goat in the old covenant. As the hours went by, our sin began to completely fill Him up. Only a God such as He could ever take on this much sin. This awesome Man who never sinned became pure sin so that we could be sinless through Him. So not only did He take the brutal beating and death for us all, He took all of our sins upon Himself as well. Again, this was a punishment that was meant for us, not Him.

For God the Father, the worst was yet to come. Aside from having to watch His only Son be tortured and killed, God had to go through a torture that was equally as painful, if not worse. Because of the sin that Jesus took on, God had to treat His Son like any other sinner that ever lived. He had to give Jesus the ultimate punishment for sin. This consequence was death and total separation from God. Again, the glory of God is much too incredible to be in the presence of sin. The only reason that Jesus could be in the physical presence of all that sin was because He laid down His true divine power and came to earth as a lowly human. We read in Hebrews 2:9, "*But we see Jesus, who was made a little lower than the angels, for the suffering of death...*"

Jesus had never been separated from His Father until this point. In John 8:29, Jesus tells us, "*And He who sent me is with Me. The Father has not left Me alone...*" The Father never had to deal with leaving His Son alone to die like this, but when the sin came into His body, He had to remove Himself from Jesus. For the first time, there was that wall of sin that separated Jesus from His Father. And what a wall of separation it was. There had never been anyone who would have as much sin as Christ took upon the cross that day. With loud sobbing, God had to remove the one thing that was keeping Jesus together, His presence. As God reluctantly pulled away from His Son, a loud yell came from out of the mouth of Jesus as He felt His Father leaving Him. We read in Matthew 27:46 that He cried out, "...*My God, My God, why have You forsaken Me?*" But Jesus didn't cry out this painful statement in the Aramaic language that He normally spoke in, as though He was speaking to everyone around Him. This was the worst moment ever in the infinite history of Jesus' life. At this exact moment, no one else existed in Jesus' mind except for Him and His Father. This was a very personal cry for God that was spoken in the original Hebrew language like His Jewish forefathers spoke. The actual words that screamed from His bleeding and swollen mouth were, "... Eli, Eli Sabachtani?" It was these same Hebrew words that Kind David had heard and seen in a prophetic vision of Jesus' crucifixion a thousand years before it ever happened (Psalms 22). This was a very desperate yell of loneliness that again proves how human and how broken Jesus really was. Upon hearing these words, God's sobbing now turned into wailing tears as He had to let His only Son die alone. It was probably that very moment that the trembling rage of Almighty God caused the earth to shake and the rocks to split as He wept (Matt. 27:51). Could any loving father possibly stay calm through the brutal murder of his son? Could any loving father forsake his son in such a time of need as this? The love that God had for us and the sacrifice to save us was more than we can ever fully understand.

    The worst part of this entire plan of salvation wasn't the physical abuse that Jesus took. It was the loneliness and the mental anguish that both He and God went through. At the point when Jesus needed Him the most, God had to abandon Him. At the point when God needed His Son the most, He had to let Him go. It was that moment that Jesus expressed the full capability of His love for us all. This was our penalty to pay, not His. We all should have been on that cross, not Him.

I always wondered why Jesus *had* to die such a brutal death. I wondered why God couldn't just snap His fingers and make everything all right. Then I realized God's Word tells us how the wages (or the consequence) of sin is death (Rom 6:23). As I said earlier, God had to give the punishment of death for our sins, otherwise He wouldn't be just. Then it was as though Jesus, who was with God from the beginning (John 1:1-2), just stepped up and said "Father, let me go down and die in their place. Let Me be separated from You. That way You can still punish sin with death and be just, and We can offer a way to those who choose Us." So, Jesus never *had* to die and go through all that torture. But, if He hadn't then we would be required the eternal death that we should have received according to God's law. What a crime it is not to love this Man for what He's done for us.

So there's Jesus, now just barely alive. He's had most of His flesh ripped off, He's nailed to a cross, He's been filled with an immeasurable amount of sin, and to top it off, His Father had to leave Him helpless and alone. Satan was in his glory as Jesus looked up to Heaven and gave up His last breath.

Satan was sure that he'd prevented Eve's Seed from defeating him. I'm sure that there was a brief celebration in hell between Satan and all of his angels and evil spirits. The party was cut to a complete halt, however, when they all saw Christ descending down into the very source of all sin—hell. The Spirit of Jesus didn't go straight down into Paradise to be with the rest of the righteous people who were in waiting. Jesus had much bigger plans. You see, Satan didn't know that Jesus died to be the sacrifice for all mankind. He didn't know that *through* His death, Jesus would be filled with the sins of all the ages. When Jesus virtually became the biggest sinner ever by boring our sins, it was a very important key to God's plan of salvation. The sins of mankind enabled Him to go straight into the heart of hell, where Satan's base of operation was, instead of going straight to Paradise, the waiting place for the righteous. In Revelation 1:18, Jesus tells us "*...I have the keys of Hades* (hell) *and of Death.*" We know from Hebrews 2:14 that through Jesus' death, "*...He might destroy him who had the power of death, that is, the devil...*" The only way to destroy Satan and take these keys from him is to confront him directly. If Jesus had gone into Paradise first, He wouldn't have been able to cross over that great gulf to get these keys of Hades. Scripture gives us enough information to see that He had to defeat Satan first, and then He could set the captives next door free. In fact, Peter reaffirms this point in Acts 2:31, when he quotes King David foreseeing, "... *the resurrection of the Christ, that His soul was not left in Hades...* " In order for Jesus' soul to be left in Hades, it had to *be* in Hades to begin with.

X. Jesus Confronts Satan

Picture this scene with me for a moment, if you will. As Jesus dies this terrible and lonely death, there were roaring cheers from all of the demons and evil angels who were once cast out of Heaven. There were also the angels who were imprisoned by God because of the corrupt generations of "giants" that were designed to keep Jesus from coming (1st Pet 3:18–20). They were all cheering and celebrating with Satan, their leader. Slowly, the cheering became quieter and quieter. As those foul beings looked around to see why the rest of them stopped cheering, they noticed many of them looking up. When all of the evil spirits finally caught on and looked up, a complete and dark silence came over all of them. Their smiles and laughter instantly turned into a confused look of desperation. The shocking sight that they were in awe of was the Son of God descending right down in the midst of them (Eph. 4:9). I can almost see the bold and powerful look on Jesus' face as He stands there in front of the devil. His very presence causes everyone there to shake and tremble with fear. They remember His awesome power and glory from the time when they were all in Heaven together. Even Satan knows that his reign of terror is about to take a big hit and that he is also subject to the authority of Jesus. All of these evil spirits, the devil, and even hell were created by this very same Person for the purpose of getting rid of sin. As Jesus slowly walked right up to Satan, it makes me wish that I was there to see the fear and humiliation that the devil felt in front of everyone. I think about the first words that came out of Jesus' mouth. I would imagine that He said something like this:

"Get down on your face before Me while I remove from you the very thing that has kept Me away from My people. That is, your keys to Death and Hades. In return, I am going to leave with you all of the sin that I brought with Me from all the ages of the world." As Jesus spoke these words, all the sin that He took from the cross left Him and was dispersed throughout hell. As Satan shamefully submits to the authority of Jesus and gets down on his face, I can picture Jesus stomping on his head as He leans down to rip the keys out of his hand (Gen. 3:15, Rev. 1:18). Since these keys were for locking and unlocking death and Hell, Jesus now had a way to cross through that great gulf that separated Hell from Paradise (Luke 16:26). Christ now had the keys to go and set all of those captives free. Jesus continued to speak: "For now, your defeat is only in part because mankind still has the free will to sin, but the days are coming when all of My saints shall be glorified and incorruptible. After this, death will be swallowed up in victory (1st Cor. 15:54), and you will be cast into a lake of fire and brimstone where you will be tormented day and night forever (Rev. 20:10). From this day on, you will no longer have authority over anyone that chooses Me (1st John 4:1). No longer will you hold captive those who have lived and died under the covenant of My Father."

As Christ leaves this disgusting place, He does something very satisfying. 1 Peter 3:18–20 tells us that when Jesus was put to death, He went and preached to the spirits in prison who were formerly disobedient in the days of Noah. These imprisoned spirits were once the same evil angels who infected all of humanity, except Noah's family, with that satanic gene (Gen. 6). After God flooded the earth, He locked up their evil spirits in Hell. Before Christ left Hell, He went in front of all these prisoners and proclaimed His victory to them. He wanted to be sure they all knew that their attempt to keep Him from coming had failed and that God reigns.

XI. He Set the Captives Free

After He had done these things, Jesus was now free of our sin. He had taken the power and the keys over death and Hell. He then proceeded to cross that great gulf that separated Hell from Paradise.

This would have been impossible before, but now Jesus had made a way.

At some point in that same day, we know that He did cross over to Paradise to be joined with all of the righteous ones who had died under the obedience of God's Law. Jesus had kept the promise that He made to the thief who died on the cross next to Him when He told him, "*...Assuredly, I say to you, **today** you will be with me in **Paradise***" (Luke 23:43). Since we know His body was dead and in the tomb for three days, then this proves it had to have been His Spirit that was awake and busy during this time.

Now the plan of salvation was almost complete. The hardest part of it was over. All that Jesus had to do now was to relax and allow all the saints in Paradise to build Him back up in worship until the third day. The Bible doesn't mention it, but I can almost picture those captive saints falling to their faces to worship the Son of God in their very presence. What a treat for them all to realize that they were all going to be rejoined with their Creator very soon forevermore in Heaven.

Jesus told His disciples and others that He would rise on the third day, but they didn't fully understand why. In the same manner that God was careful not to give too many clues about how Jesus was going to defeat the devil, Jesus wasn't going to let the devil know that He was planning on dying, either. I'm sure that Satan was snooping in His business every chance he could to try to figure out the strategy that Jesus was going to use, but He was careful with His words. None of the disciples really understood what Jesus meant concerning His death until it actually happened. But just as He predicted, it came to pass. He died on a Friday afternoon. His body went into a tomb for three days, while His Spirit went down into Hell, and then He crossed over to Paradise for those three days; then He rose from the dead. This is why we must trust in Him. He knows what He's doing.

XII. He Is Risen

Sunday morning, His Spirit rejoined with His body that had been lying in the tomb. Only now, God had changed Jesus' old body into a new, glorified body that is not of this world. As the angels of God caused the stone that sealed the tomb to be rolled away, Jesus rose up and walked out (Matt. 28:2). Just as heartbreaking as it was to see His Son go to the cross to die, it was the greatest thrill ever for God to see Him rise up after being victorious over death, Hell, and the grave. Now the wait was over because it really was finished. Every task, great and small, which the Father asked of His Son had been accomplished. There was nothing in God's plan that Christ didn't fulfill. Jesus went from being God, to being pure sin, and now He was back on His way to glory again.

When Jesus' Spirit ascended from Paradise back to the earth on the third day, He brought all of the captive souls of the dead saints with Him to be taken to Heaven and await the final resurrection (1st Thess. 4:13–18). Today, Paradise (or Abraham's Bosom) is empty because we have no need of it. We have the real thing now—Heaven. Paradise was a place to wait for redemption, and thanks to Jesus' sacrifice, we can now be redeemed from the original sin that we were born into and also the sins we have committed by choice. Now through Christ we will instantly be with the Father when we die.

At Jesus' death, God shook the earth, and certain tombs and graves were opened. These belonged to some of the saints who had recently died. God raised these people from the dead, just like Jesus raised Lazarus from the dead (John 11). These saints went into Jerusalem and "...*appeared to many*" (Matt 27:52–53). What a powerful testimony this was to show the Jews and the Romans that they really did kill the Son of God.

The next chapter will explain how the Holy Spirit consecrates God's entire plan for our salvation.

3 A New Birth Through the Holy Spirit

Now we've seen God's plan from the very beginning. We've seen how it came about and why it had to happen in order to save us from the original sin of Adam as well as our own sins. In order for us believers to be united together in the Lord, it is important to understand *how* this new salvation works. Once you see exactly what happens when you are "born again," then you will understand why all of Heaven rejoices over each and every soul that gets saved (Luke 15:10). You will also be able to know Jesus on a more personal level because He becomes the object of your faith and hope. When you know what it means to be "saved" or "born again," then you will have such a greater appreciation for the suffering that He went through for all of us.

Most of the different churches see eye-to-eye on the subject of being born again. However, for the ones who ignore it or teach it falsely, this chapter is dedicated solely to this new birth. Again, the purpose for this chapter is that in order to understand Bible doctrines, we must first have a solid understanding of the basic principles of God's plan of salvation.

I. A Personal Gift from Jesus

If we go back to the evening of the day that Christ was resurrected, we can see the new covenant in action for the first time. John 20:19–22 tells us that Jesus appeared in front of His disciples (except Thomas, and of course, Judas) and showed them His hands and His side. They saw His scars and realized that it really was Jesus and that He truly did rise from the dead just like Mary Magdalene had told them (John 20:18). The disciples already knew that Jesus was the Son of God. They already knew that they were born into a sinful body and needed Him to redeem them of their sins. Now, for the first time, the disciples saw that Christ had risen from the dead, and He had the scars to prove that it was really His body. Believing in these three things are the requirements that anyone needs to receive salvation under the new covenant (Rom. 10:9). Since the disciples had believed all of these three truths for the first time, Jesus breathed on them and said, "... *Receive the Holy Spirit*" (John 20:22). Just like the Holy Spirit breathed life into Adam, Jesus breathed a new life into the disciples by the same Holy Spirit. Now they had a way to reunite with the Lord forever. The solution was not just to be born of flesh and blood but to be born "again," or reborn by the Holy Spirit. In John 3:5, Jesus tells us that in order to have eternal life with Him, we must be born of "water" and "Spirit." There are only two types of births in a Christian's life—physical birth and their spiritual birth into Christ. If for no other reason than the process of elimination, the "water" birth must refer to the physical birth because the spirit birth can only mean a birth by the Holy Spirit. Some people link this "water birth" in John 3:5 to water baptism. This is untrue, and it is taken totally out of context. The water birth refers to the water that your mother carried you in as an unborn child. When your mother's "water broke," you were then born shortly after. This is the way the Jews worded this event in this time period. If you read the entire third chapter of John, then you will clearly see what Jesus is trying to tell Nicodemas. Jesus explained to him that in order to have eternal life, you not only had to be physically born (born of flesh), but you must be born of the Spirit also. Since our bodies were tainted from the original sin of Adam, God came up with this new plan that still keeps our corrupt bodies in the world after death, while our new Spirit takes our soul up to be with Him forever. The things of the world belong to the ruler of this world—the devil. But the things that are of the Spirit, like born again Christians, belong to God.

The Bible tells us that flesh and blood cannot inherit the Kingdom of God (1st Cor. 15:50), so if we want to live eternally with the Lord, then we must be reborn of the Spirit. This is the main difference between any old covenant with God and the one we have now. Since Jesus came, the Holy Spirit has sealed this covenant up for us once and for all. James 2:26 informs us that, "... *the body without the spirit is dead...*" There are a lot of dead people walking around today who need to be Spirit born. I'm not talking about ghosts. I'm talking about the millions of unsaved people in the world who are still dead in their sins. The Holy Spirit is like the vehicle that will one day transport your soul to Heaven. Without the Spirit, you will have no mode of transportation and no chance for eternal life.

Jesus' disciples were the first ones to receive this incredible gift of being "born again" under the new covenant. This was a personal, hand-delivered gift that was strictly for His disciples at that time. Everyone else had to wait until the Day of Pentecost, when Jesus ascended back into Heaven. Only then could He send the fullness of the Holy Spirit down to the earth to be the final link in God's plan of salvation. Jesus Himself said to His disciples, "... *It is to your advantage that I go away; for if I do not go away, the Helper* (the Holy Spirit) *will not come to you; but if I depart, I will send Him to you.*" (John 16:7).

II. The Role of the Holy Spirit

The role of the Holy Spirit is to be the omnipresence of the Godhead. This means that no matter where someone is in the world, or no matter what time of the day it is, the Holy Spirit is ready to offer the gift of salvation to anyone that accepts Jesus as their Lord and Savior. We read in Ephesians 2:18, "*For through Him we both have access by one Spirit to the Father.*" The Holy Spirit also plays the role of a divine "Remote Control," if I can say that reverently. Since we know that Jesus is at the right hand of the Father in Heaven (Rom. 8:34), then we must realize that the Holy Spirit is the Agent through which God works on the earth. When Jesus was on the earth, He could only be in one place at a time. From Heaven, He could be everywhere at once through the power of the Holy Spirit (which is why it was to the disciples' advantage that Jesus left [John 16:7]). This is the Jesus that lives today. Now He's just waiting to offer eternal life to anyone who believes in what He did for us.

Salvation, just like anything else, requires all three People of the Godhead, or Trinity. The Father is the Creator who decided that He wanted to redeem mankind. The Son executed the will of the Father through His death and resurrection. The Holy Spirit sealed up God's plan of salvation (Eph. 1:13), and now He waits for invitations to draw people to the Father.

Let's get back to Jesus and His disciples. After they received the Holy Ghost, Jesus spent a few more weeks with them. There were forty days in all that He stayed there for them after His resurrection. He gave the disciples some last minute preparations concerning the mission ahead. They were told to go and spread the Good News about how Christ redeemed all who would accept Him (Mark 16:15). On the fortieth day after His resurrection, Jesus told the disciples not to leave but to wait for the "... *Promise of the Father* ..." (Acts 1:4–5). Remember, the disciples already received this Promise (Luke 24:49). Jesus was telling them that in "... *not many days from now* ..." the Holy Spirit would be available for everyone else and to wait for this to happen. The Promise of the Father is our gift of eternal life through our faith in Christ. That promise is for us, our children, and to all who are afar off (Acts 2:39). Jesus also told them that He would pour out His Spirit upon His believers, and it would give His people supernatural power to be a mighty witness concerning Him (Acts 1:8).

III. The Day of Pentecost—The Beginning of a New Age

After He spoke these things, Jesus was taken up into Heaven. The disciples went to the upper room, where about one hundred twenty of them prayed in unity for ten days straight (Acts 1:13–15). On the Day of Pentecost, fifty days after Jesus' resurrection and ten days after He ascended back to Heaven, the Holy Spirit came down in all fullness. The era of the church, which the Prophet Joel called "... *the last days* ..." had begun (Acts 2:16–21). Joel not only predicted that all who believe in the Lord will be saved, but that they may also receive supernatural powers from the Holy Spirit to be a more effective witness. For the first time since The Fall of Man, the entire human race had an opportunity to be rejoined with our Creator. On this day, God's plan of salvation was completely at hand by the coming of the Holy Spirit. Just as Adam infected man kind with sin, the Holy Spirit came to disinfect us from those sins.

From the Day of Pentecost until now, God gives us the honor of having eternal life with Him. All that we have to do is believe and accept that Jesus made that way possible for us. In Adam's day, God made the choice easy for him, but he chose poorly. God gave him one tiny command with a huge consequence if he disobeyed. Now God is giving *us* a no-brainer just like He gave Adam in the Garden of Eden. If we will just believe in Jesus as our Savior, we will inherit eternal life in Heaven instead of eternal torture in hell. It's like winning a billion dollar lottery, and all you have to do now is turn in your ticket. God makes it so easy for us, but He stops short of forcing us to choose Him. There are still so many people who don't cash in their inheritance that has already been paid for by the blood of Jesus. There are many "Adams" in the world who abuse the free will that God gave them.

IV. Separated From God

You will notice as you read through the Gospels that Jesus was never spiritually separated from the Father until the very end of His life (John 8:29). This is exactly the reason why He could cast out demons in an instant (Mark 5:8). This is why He had the power to raise the dead, heal the sick, and cause the wind to settle (Mark 4:39). Jesus was never born into sin, nor did He sin by choice during His 33-plus years on the earth. It is our sin that has always separated us from God. Isaiah 59:1–2 confirms this by telling us, *"Behold, the Lord's hand is not shortened, That it cannot save; Nor His ear heavy that it cannot hear. But your iniquities have separated you from your God; And your sins have hidden His face from you, So that He will not hear."* Sin is what keeps God from hearing our prayers and our praises to Him. Sin hides His face from us. Since Jesus was completely without sin, He had a direct line of communication with His Father. It might seem that Jesus had an advantage that we can't have, but on the contrary, He has given us the same opportunity that He had. Not to mention that Hebrews 4:15 tells us Jesus *"… was in all points tempted as we are, yet without sin."*

Since we were born into a sinful body, we must be reborn into a spiritual birth. The result of this Spirit birth is that we can be spiritually joined with God the Father just like Jesus was when He was human. This is not a birth that can be seen with human eyes. That's why the world doesn't understand the ways of the Lord; they try to look through their worldly, human eyes instead of spiritual eyes. Nonetheless, this birth is necessary to continue living with God after the physical body dies (1st Cor. 15:44). This is how we as sinful humans can be found righteous in God's eyes. As for Christ never sinning, we can ask God and those who we've sinned against for forgiveness, and it will be as though we never sinned in the first place, as long as we turn away from that sinful way of life (Jer. 31:34). So Jesus shows us how to be born again and how to live a life apart from sin. The stricter we follow these instructions, the smaller the separation will be between us and God. At one point in Peter's life, he was so close to the Lord that sick people were laid in the streets just so Peter's shadow could pass over them and be healed (Acts 5:15–16). We can all have that closeness with God through the power of the Holy Spirit. It just depends on how closely we live according to the standards given to us in the Bible.

The Bible tells us that many people are destroyed because of the lack of knowledge (Hos. 4:6). If they knew God's Word of Truth, then they would turn away from their sins and accept Him as our Way out. This is the reason that God laid it on my heart to write this teaching about His plan from start to finish. The lack of this teaching has caused many cults to pop up in the world. Some of these false religions believe that Jesus never existed before Mary bore Him as a human being. Some believe that He was not the only begotten Son of God, or that He was not killed and resurrected. Any one of these beliefs takes you out of the realm of Christianity. Again, in order to be "Spirit born," you must confess that Jesus Christ truly is your Savior as the Son of the living God. More importantly, you have to really believe it in your heart. If you have a real hard time believing, then ask God to help you. In Matthew 7:7–8, Jesus tells us to *"Ask, and it will be given to you; seek, and you will find; knock, and it will be opened to you. "For everyone who asks receives, and he who seeks finds, and to him who knocks it will be opened."* You might be surprised at the great lengths God will go to in order to see you spend eternity with Him.

When you choose to accept Christ as your Savior, God gives us a reward that is indescribable. If we just believe the truth about Jesus, then we can look forward to an eternal life in Heaven without sickness, depression, hatred, or anything else that's ugly—*forever.* If you live your whole life for the Lord and find out after death that God wasn't real, then what have you really lost except some lusts of the flesh? But if you live your life without Jesus in it and the Bible *is* telling the truth, then you've made a mistake that will cost you torture in hell for all of eternity. Even though hell is very real, we shouldn't accept Christ out of fear of hell. We should accept Him because of the love that He has for us all. Think back to what the entire Trinity of God had to go through just to redeem us of the original sin of Adam. Are we just going to tell God, "Thanks anyway, but it's not worth it if I have to change my lifestyle"? You can live to be a hundred years old in this life, but that's not even one percent of what eternal life is. Your free will choices in this "one percent life" dictate where you're going to spend your eternal "ninety-nine percent life." If Heaven does become your home, then your actions here on earth also determine how great you will be in Heaven and how many treasures you will have stored up when you get there (Matt. 6:19, 1st Cor. 5:10). I personally look forward to the day in Heaven when I can offer all of my treasures back to Jesus for the awesome sacrifice He made for me. What a pity it would be if I had nothing to offer Him to show my gratitude. Regardless of what we believe, we all will spend the rest of eternity wishing we did more for the Lord. Our time now is way too valuable to waste away on worldly things.

V. An Opportunity for Salvation

If you're learning about who Jesus really is for the first time, then my prayers have been answered. I thank God for going through me to reach other people because I can do nothing without Him. I want you to know that He isn't just our God after we die, He's our God now. He wants us to prosper in every way possible as long as we keep Him first in our lives. He can heal you physically, mentally, and spiritually. He wants to help us with our problems and be a part of our everyday lives. But He also wants us to mature and learn without spoiling us. That is the reason He created man in the first place. He is the best insurance policy there ever has been. Your problems are now His problems if you put your faith and trust in Him. If you choose not to believe in Him, then at least teach your children about Jesus and let them decide for themselves whether they want eternal life or death. We have no right to rob anyone of what Christ has done for us.

If you've never been born of the Spirit and you want to, then let me give you some advice. Whether it's at church, or at a water baptism, or wherever you are right now, just go to a place where you can focus on the Lord. Close your eyes and lift your hands to Heaven. Confess to the Lord out loud that you are a sinner both by birth and by choice. Tell God that you truly believe in your heart that Jesus Christ is His Son and that He died for you so you could be free from your sins. Ask God to forgive you for those sins that have already been paid for by Jesus on that cross. Finally, ask God to send the Holy Spirit into your life to give you a new birth in Christ. If you pray this from your heart *and truly believe* it, then the most incredible miracle ever will take place in your life (Rom. 10:9–10). These are the words that God has waited your whole life to hear. He didn't create you to live 80 or 100 years here on earth. He created you so you can live with him forever.

Think about how lost you would be without this incredible gift of salvation. Imagine that instead of an eternity in a devil's hell, you will spend eternity with your Creator, living the glorious life we were created to live. Imagine that even if everyone in your life has let you down and you have screwed up so many times that you lost count, God is still running to you with His arms wide open (Luke 15). He wants to be rejoined with you, but He has just been waiting for you to let Him. You may feel an uncontrollable urge to cry. If so, let your tears cleanse your past. You may even feel a tingling that starts in your feet and works its way up. This is God filling you with the Holy Spirit. Everyone has their own unique experience with salvation, so don't feel like yours has to be the same as someone else's. Please understand that accepting Christ as your Savior is not the total experience of living a Christian life, it's only the opening door. Living a Christian life is experienced on the other side of that door through our witness and our obedience to God's Word. This is our road to purity. God takes us and cleanses us from our sinful ways. A great way to see how God has worked in your life is to mark your spiritual growth every few months. You may notice that you haven't been cursing as much, or maybe you can't lie anymore because it makes you feel like garbage inside. Maybe you used to be big on gossiping with your co-workers, but now you see the good in those people that you once spoke badly about. Whatever the case, there should always be some growth. If there isn't, then maybe you should seriously seek God and ask Him to put you back on that path. In Romans 12:1–2, Paul says to "... *present your bodies a living sacrifice, holy acceptable to God, which is your **reasonable** service. And do not be conformed to this world...*" For the great lengths that God went to redeem us, it is **reasonable** for us to return the favor to Him by trying to live a holy life.

Salvation is a gift that is free for you because it has already been paid for by Jesus' death. You don't have to earn it like a paycheck. It would be like taking a trip far away. You go to the only hotel around and find out there are no rooms available. There is no price that you can pay to get a room because they're all taken. A man named Jesus comes up to you and your family and says "I have paid for a room, and I want your family to have it." All you would have to do is use the name of Jesus to get the hotel room because it is reserved in His name. This same principal is what it takes for us to have eternal life in Heaven.

Don't make the same mistake that some people make by thinking they have to change *before* they accept Jesus as their Lord. When you give your heart to Him, ask Him to supply you with supernatural power from on high to help you overcome the obstacles that separate you from Him (Acts 1:8). It is a must for every new "born again" Christian to pray every day and ask Him to help you stay on fire for Jesus. This is a very vulnerable time for you. This is a time in which the devil will try everything in the book to get you to slip back into your sinful life. The moment you stop asking God to help you get through this time, Satan will take that opportunity to bombard you with everything in his arsenal. He doesn't want you going to Heaven, and he especially doesn't want you to take others with you. Until you get God's Word anchored deep into your heart and mind, you desperately need to pray that God helps you get past this stage.

Satan is under complete submission to the Lord. If he could, he would reach up and kill every one of us. He hates God and all of His creation, but there's nothing that he can directly do to harm Him. The only way that the devil can get back at God is to try to destroy us, His children. He has been the source of temptation from the beginning, and he's very good at what he does. If you or someone you know has a hard time believing in God, or if you have been tricked into thinking that the Bible is just a book full of fairy tales, then Satan has done his job. We know from 1st Timothy 4:1 that, *"... in the latter times some will depart from the faith, giving heed to deceiving spirits and doctrines of demons..."* These people will find out one day how badly they were deceived whether they believe it now or not. However, if you have been born of the Spirit, then you have the power within you to overcome the devil. 1st John 4:4 tells us "... *He* (God) *who is in you is greater than he* (Satan) *who is in the world...*" You cannot expect to see the world from God's eye view without the Spirit of God living in you. As long as Jesus is in your heart, then Satan is no match for you. Without Christ in your heart, then you are no match for Satan. He will destroy you without you ever knowing it. He is a master deceiver. Just look at the forty-five million babies that were aborted in the past thirty plus years. Satan has convinced these pregnant women that it isn't a baby they're aborting. It's just "excess tissue." You will understand how deceiving the devil is the first time you try to debate the deity of God with someone who doesn't believe in Him. We as Christians may never be able to prove the truth about the Gospel with facts and reason, but I promise you that by accepting Christ, you will know in your heart He is real. That's true faith.

I've heard some people say, "I haven't accepted Jesus or the devil.

I'm just staying out of it." If you think this way, then I've got news for you; if you don't accept the reality of what Jesus went through in order to redeem you of your sins and ask Him to be your Savior, then Satan has chosen you already, whether you want him to or not. If you don't choose Jesus as your Savior, then by default you choose the devil. There is no in between.

4 The Effects of "Overshooting"

So far, I've just laid down the foundation for the rest of the book. Again, the purpose up to this point was to teach the whole plan that God had for mankind so we can better understand why we believe the way we do. I hope that everyone understands now what salvation is, why we need it, and how we can acquire it. If you have just finished reading the first three chapters and you gave your heart to the Lord for the first time, I would highly recommend that you get into a Bible believing church and start growing in God's Word with other Christians. Also, stay away from the people and places that bring out the worst in you, if at all possible. I would also recommend that you start to read about Jesus' life in an easy-to-read translation of the Bible. For everyone else, we're going to look at what we should and should not do when we study Bible doctrine.

The first no-no that I want to talk about is what I call "overshooting." Overshooting is when someone over-emphasizes a particular subject in the Bible and turns it into something that God never originally meant for it to be. I'm going to give you two examples to show you what I mean. Afterwards, I hope you will be able to identify what it is and how to avoid it.

I. Mary, the Mother of Jesus

The first example of overshooting that I want to discuss pertains to Mary, the mother of Jesus. For centuries, Mary has been prayed to, worshipped, and thought of as a link between man and Jesus by many people. This is a tradition that has been held by different religions and churches throughout the world. However, this tradition strongly over-emphasizes what God had originally intended.

Mary was never meant to be the subject of worship or prayer, and I'll explain why.

From the time that Adam and Eve were created until about four thousand years later, Mary never existed. She was thought of and prophesied of (Isaiah 7:14), but she wasn't around when the earth was created like Jesus was. Mary might have given birth to Christ as a human being on the earth, but it was Christ who created Mary in the first place (John 1:1–3). When Mary was born, she was born into the original sin of Adam, just like we all were. Remember, all men and women alike are born into a sinful body, but the original sin of Adam is only passed on from our biological father. Jesus avoided the original sin of Adam by being conceived by the Holy Spirit. Thus His sacrifice was sufficient for all of us because of His purity.

Mary had a biological father named Heli. We know this from the two different genealogies in the Bible. Since Matthew 1:1–16 and Luke 3:23–38 have different names in their genealogies from King David's sons on to Joseph (the step-father of Jesus), then we must accept that one is the lineage of Joseph, and the other is Mary's line. The book of Luke lists Mary's lineage all of the way back to Adam. But since she was a woman, and women did not dictate the genealogical records in the Jewish culture, they put Joseph's name in her place. We can see that this is true by comparing Joseph's father in both accounts. Matthew 1:16 tells us, *"And Jacob begot Joseph the husband of Mary, of whom was born Jesus who is called Christ."* Luke 3:23 tells us that Jesus was the supposed son of Joseph, and that Joseph was the son of *Heli*. Since Jacob *begot* Joseph in Matthew 1:16, then he must be his biological father because you can only be begotten from one biological father. Heli would have been Joseph's father-in-law—Mary's father. This is why Joseph could have been called the *son* of Heli, but not the *begotten* son of Heli. By putting these scriptures together, we can get the correct line of Joseph and Mary's genealogy.

The point of this explanation was to show that Mary born into sin from her father just like everyone else has been, and she needed to be redeemed for that sin just like everyone else did. If we assume that Mary or anyone else was never born into a sinful body, then it takes away from the importance of who Christ is. Before Mary died, she had to have been born again by the Holy Spirit, just like all believers are under the new covenant. Since Mary is no different than other Christians in the world today in that respect, then why should she be worshipped like a god? That also goes for anyone else that has been used as an object of worship, not just Mary. Everyone else needs to be redeemed by the only One without original sin or intentional sin—Jesus Christ. This fact sets Jesus apart from anyone who has ever been regarded as a god. No other god from any other religion can claim this divine truth. Everyone needs Jesus in order to be saved!

Today, Jesus sits at the right hand of the Father in Heaven. You'd have to be crazy to think that He submits to Mary from there as He did when He was a child on earth. Matthew 28:18 tells us that, *"...All authority has been given to Me in Heaven and on earth."* You couldn't possibly believe that after Jesus had been with the Father since the beginning of time, God, as well as His Son, was going to later create a mortal, human woman that Jesus would have to submit to from then on. This idea strongly belittles our Lord and Savior.

Mary had an awesome calling on her life, which was to fulfill a specific duty. She gave a miracle birth to Someone that laid aside His glorious and authoritative life and went under total reliance of His Father. Hebrews 2:9 tells us, *"But we see Jesus, who was made a little lower than the angels..."* It was this humble human being that Mary bore, not the dynamic superpower that created the Heavens and the earth. If Mary would have been the mother of Jesus from the beginning of time, then she'd be more than worthy to be worshipped and prayed to. If this were the case, then she would be part of the godhead. The reality is that Mary spent about 33 years being His human mother, but Jesus will be her Lord for the rest of eternity.

Mary and Joseph had four boys and at least two girls after they had Jesus (Matt. 13:55–56). If Mary was to be worshipped and prayed to, then do these other sons and daughters deserve the same? It was the conception by the Holy Spirit that made the baby Jesus divine, not Mary or Joseph. In fact, Mary's contribution was responsible for Jesus' human weakness. That physical human body that Mary gave birth to doesn't exist anymore. God took His earthly body and changed it into a glorified body before it ever saw corruption or decay. This was referred to by the great King David in Acts 2:27, when he said, "*... nor will You allow Your Holy One* (Jesus) *to see corruption.*" Acts 2:31 confirms that David was referring to the *flesh* of Jesus that didn't see corruption (decay). What this is saying here is that the physical side of Christ that Mary gave birth to has been changed into a heavenly glorified body that doesn't have the weaknesses of humanity. So the human side of Jesus that Mary contributed to us, as special and as important as it was, does not exist anymore. Only the memories and the history of His earthly body exist.

The Father, the Son, and the Holy Spirit make up a single Godhead that can be everywhere at the same time. Mary is not a part of this Trinity. Since she's not a part of this omnipresent godhead, then how could she be everywhere at once to hear all of the prayers to her? Somewhere down the line, Mary's role was strongly overexaggerated as being deity or "god-like." I know that if Mary could come down to earth and tell you this herself, she would. It wouldn't be her will for us to distort God's Word. In fact, in her own words, she thanks God for still regarding her as a maidservant, even in her lowly state (Luke 1:48).

Having said all of that, Mary truly was blessed among all women. It is important not to overshoot her role as Jesus' human mother, but it is equally important that we give her the acknowledgement that she deserves. She will always be the woman that God used to physically manifest His Son into the world. No one besides her can ever say that they carried the soul of the Messiah in her womb. Nobody can ever take that away from her. Because of this, there will never be a more blessed woman on the earth. Because of this, Mary was worthy to be called "Mother" by the disciples (John 19:27). She will get to go through all of eternity having experienced that wonderful miracle birth.

II. Speaking In Tongues
Another subject in the Bible that I see being strongly overshot in

many churches today is "speaking in tongues." In chapter 8, we will plug this doctrine into the *Bible formula* so we can let the Word of God explain this gift for us from a doctrinal standpoint. For now, we're just going to identify how the gift of tongues is both overshot and under-emphasized in the church.

Many churches and even families have been split apart because of the misunderstanding of this spiritual gift. On the one side, you've got people and churches that will go as far as saying that if you don't speak in tongues, then you won't go to Heaven. Many other churches who do believe in spiritual gifts will teach that unless you initially speak in tongues, then you can't possibly be filled with or empowered by the Holy Ghost. These circumstances are at one end of the spectrum. The other end is quite the opposite. These are the churches that completely remove the spiritual gifts from the Bible. Some even claim that speaking in tongues and prophesying is of the devil. These denominations believe that the gifts of the Spirit that the Bible mentions were just to get the church started and are not for today.

I believe there are many reasons for these different opinions. One major problem occurs when a church or a denomination exalts the gift of speaking in tongues so highly that it makes those who don't have it feel left out and unworthy. Once this happens, the result is often one of two things. The first result is speaking false tongues or false prophesies. The people that make these bad choices are usually seeking attention or just trying to fit in with what they feel are "higher level" Christians in the church. They don't want to be looked at as being inferior or any less of a believer than everyone else, so they just speak in tongues the way they hear everyone else do it, even though it's not from the Lord. Some people actually believe they have the gift when their false spiritual language starts sounding like the others in the church. This causes a chain reaction of falseness from generation to generation and from church to church. Unfortunately, this result will often chase people out of these churches and into churches that do not believe in spiritual gifts. They leave because they've seen so much faking that they wonder if everyone who speaks in tongues is faking also. They begin to question whether or not any of the gifts of the Spirit are really true. This is why God strongly warns against false prophesying (2nd Peter 2).

Too often, false tongues and false prophesies are allowed just because nobody wants to offend the person by calling it out as being false for the fear of losing the church member (and possibly their tithe). Or maybe the thought of receiving a word from the Lord in service is more important to the pastor and to the congregation than not receiving a word. Thus even if the pastor knows it wasn't from God, he will let it continue for the sake of the congregation's confidence and for the convenience it brings to edify their church in a fleshly, man-pleasing sort of way. It kind of makes people feel more spiritual, regardless if it's right or wrong.

Other people leave these churches because they tried to receive this gift that is often said to be "absolutely necessary" and have never been successful, so they feel like a spiritual failure. I have personally seen Christians sob because they thought God didn't love them when they couldn't receive this gift after trying and praying for years. *When the gift of tongues is exalted, then the expectation of receiving this gift is exalted also.* In fact, I've seen and heard of churches trying many different techniques to get people to speak in tongues. Sometimes people will tell you to just start speaking in a different language or make goofy sounds. Maybe they'll dim the lights down or shake you while praying to try to get this gift out of you. Maybe they will even start playing the music louder and louder to build up the moment. I certainly mean no disrespect, but I don't believe that God needs our help giving someone a spiritual gift as long as it's His will for us to have it. The apostles Peter and Paul never used any "techniques" to fill people with the Holy Spirit. They knew that the Holy Spirit didn't need their help.

From what I've seen, there are a couple of reasons for this misconstrued belief of the gift of tongues. The first reason is that when God truly does pour this gift into someone, the experience is so exhilarating that people think it's the *only* way you can be filled with the Holy Spirit. However, the same could be said about the other gifts of the Spirit if we all would let God distribute His spiritual gifts as He wills, not as we will (1st Cor. 12:11). Often times, this awesome experience will be coupled with the fact that speaking in other tongues is physical proof that they, and others around them, can see and hear immediately. Sadly, we live in a world that will not believe unless we see proof. Thomas, one of Jesus' disciples, would not believe that Jesus had risen from the dead unless he saw Him personally with his own eyes. When Jesus confronted Thomas, He told him, "*... because you have seen Me, you have believed. Blessed are those who have not seen and yet have believed.*" (John 20:29). Jesus is trying to teach us how to have strong faith without seeing the proof all of the time. He said again in John 4:48, "*... Unless you people see signs and wonders, you will by no means believe.*"

The gifts that God gives you are not meant to show other Christians whether or not you have been filled with the Holy Ghost. They're meant to make you a supernaturally powerful witness concerning Jesus Christ (Acts 1:8). This is the one guaranteed evidence of being filled with the Holy Ghost: God will empower you supernaturally (or in a way that you could never do on your own) to be an effective witness to the world for Jesus. These are prime examples and consequences of what overshooting will do to churches.

The other side of the denominational "tongues" war is the one where churches completely remove this gift and claim that it's not for today. This false teaching is equally as wrong as speaking false tongues. The truth is that there is nowhere in the Bible where the gift of tongues is implied as being only for the beginning of the church. In fact, in Mark 16:15, Jesus commands the disciples to preach the Gospel to the world. Mark 16:17 tells us that one of the signs of believers is that they will speak with new tongues. Jesus never implies that this will only be for the beginning of the church. If you assume this, then you must also assume that the Great Commission of Mark 16:15 was only meant to get the church started also. This would also have to imply that Christians are *not* supposed to spread the Gospel anymore. If this was the case, then we shouldn't have any churches in the world.

I've heard many people who don't believe in the gift of tongues quote 1st Corinthians 13:8, where it says, "*... whether there are tongues, they will cease ...*" This is a prime example of people singling out scriptures to get the doctrine that they want. What they don't tell you is how the author, Paul, goes on to explain that there will come a time where everything that is incomplete or in part will be perfected. At that time, which refers to us being in Heaven, there will be no need for other tongues because we will all speak the same language. Paul was comparing these different things (that will one day be of no use) to love, which will never cease. That was the point Paul was making, and what a good point it is. If everybody sought after love the most, which is the greatest gift (1st Cor, 13:13), then there would be little reason for this book on breaking down divisions in the church. I've met people who loved the Lord so much that it didn't even matter whether or not they agreed with everyone else's doctrine. The love of God just pours out of these people, and that's what breaks down walls of divisions and draws others to them as well. True love like this always keeps the doors open for communication between believers, as well as unbelievers. Without love, all of your spiritual gifts mean nothing. 1st Corinthians 13:1-2 tells us, "*Though I speak with the tongues of men and of angels, but have not love... I am nothing.*"

If we look at why so many Christians fight each other over this doctrine of tongues, then we can see how the devil works us against each other. What happens is that once people have been a victim of feeling left out from the first type of church that overshoots speaking in tongues, they will then deny the gifts of the Spirit and try to distort the Bible to make it suit their hurt feelings. Maybe the reason that this gift has been so overshot in many churches was to balance out the people who have tried to put it down so much and say that it wasn't a gift for today. Just the same, maybe the ones who have tried to balance this doctrine out by putting down tongues are the same people who have witnessed so much faking and falseness. The important thing to remember is that we cannot change what the Bible says no matter how badly other churches overshoot or underemphasize a particular doctrine. The same applies to Jesus' mother, Mary. We can't put her down just to balance out the people who exalt her as a deity. We have to take each subject for what it is.

A large part of the blame for these two examples of overshooting must be put on the teachers, pastors, evangelists, and everyone else for just accepting the traditions that were passed down to them from other men and women and not having an open mind to the possibility that these traditions could be wrong. James 3:1 gives a firm warning when it says, "*My brethren, let not many of you become teachers, knowing that we shall receive a stricter judgment.*" Knowing this, I would hope that anyone who teaches Bible doctrines would not rely solely on the traditions that were handed down to them but that they would confirm all doctrines by using the entire Word of God. As long as we follow the Bible, then our judgment is guaranteed to be rewarding and not condemning. The bottom line is that there's too much human error that has been inserted into different doctrines. What we need to do more of is to stop teaching hand-me-down doctrines and start finding the one and only truth.

Please know that the main purpose of this chapter wasn't necessarily to teach about Mary or the gift of tongues. It was to identify what overshooting is and to understand the consequences of it. The purpose is to find out the truth about a certain subject in the Bible and not add to it or take anything away from it just to balance out what other churches believe. You might be able to think of a lot of subjects that have been overshot and under-emphasized. I recommend that you search these matters out with an open mind and find the truth.

The Danger Of Singling Out Scriptures 5

The best advice that I can give to anyone who reads the Bible is to pray first. Pray that God reveals His truth to your heart. Pray for understanding and wisdom. Most of all, pray that you might retain the knowledge that you're about to receive and use it to bring souls to Christ. After you've prayed, open your mind to the Holy Spirit and let Him teach you. 1st Corinthians 2:10–14 explains how the Holy Spirit that lives in us (if you're born again) teaches us the ways of God. Without the Holy Spirit inside of us, the Word of God would seem like foolishness (v. 14). Praying before you read will help keep you from misinterpreting the Bible.

There are many reasons for misunderstanding God's Word. We're going to study the common mistake of singling out Bible verses and not using them in the manner that God intended. Singling out Bible verses is one of the biggest reasons for false doctrines and church divisions. We know that God's people are destroyed for the lack of knowledge (Hos. 4:6). Today, we see that these people have such a lack of knowledge from using incomplete Bible scriptures to form a particular belief.

I. Turning Orange into Red and Yellow

God gave us His Word to give our lives direction, meaning, and understanding. It's okay to pick out certain lines from a dictionary or an encyclopedia, but the Bible is different. It must be used as a whole or as a complete resource. I would like to give an illustration to better explain this by using colors. Let's say that the Bible represents the color orange. Orange is made up of the two colors, red and yellow. Many Christians try to interpret the Bible not as being the original color of orange, but by singling out the colors that make up orange—red and yellow. If God intended us to have orange and we turn it into red and yellow, then we've changed the wholeness that God gave us in the first place. The way you extract red and yellow from orange is the same way people extract scriptures out of their original context in the Bible. God put the Bible together so that every word is where it is supposed to be. By singling out a verse and not applying it to its original place in the Bible, you take the risk of turning that particular verse into something that God never intended it to be. So many times this has created false doctrines, then different denominations in the church, and sometimes it has even created cults.

Another important factor for using scriptures in their proper text is finding the root word in the original Hebrew or Greek. Sometimes we need to search out certain words of a Scripture for ourselves with a concordance in order to dig deeper into what God really wanted us to know.

II. The Danger of Memorizing Bible Verses

Before we get into different examples of singling out scriptures, I want to talk about memorizing Bible verses. It's important to know that the authors who wrote the Bible did not write in chapters and verses. They just wrote accounts of history as the Holy Spirit inspired them to and as they witnessed them. The verse numbers were added later for reference purposes.

Many Bible readers strive to memorize scriptures. It *is* a privilege when we can direct someone to a particular verse in the Bible to give them the answers to certain questions. It's also nice to be able to quote Bible verses for certain situations in people's lives. However, there is a danger, or at least a risk involved, when memorizing Bible verses. The risk comes when a verse is quoted by itself and not plugged into its original context. Quoting a single verse can run the risk of someone else interpreting that verse incorrectly. Instead of them seeing the whole picture, they just get a small piece of the puzzle. This small piece can often be as naked as a jaybird and can easily be misinterpreted by the ones who don't know the original context that God had planned for the verse. There are some Bible verses, like John 3:16, where there is little or no danger of misusing it out of context because the verse explains itself so well. Many of the verses in the Book of Proverbs don't have this risk of being taken out of context. However, there are so many Bible verses that are misused because they have been singled out and not used the way God designed them. God inspired the authors of His Word to write *books*, not necessarily a singled out collection of verses that can distort the wholeness of the books. When we concentrate on one verse instead of the meaning of the whole chapter or even the whole book, then that verse becomes susceptible to being interpreted in a way that God never wanted. Now we've taken the color orange and made it into the red and yellow colors that it was never supposed to be.

It is so important that if we just use one or two scriptures out of the Bible, then we have to be sure that we're using it in the manner that God had planned it to be used. I would strongly encourage you not to get caught up so much in memorizing verses word for word, but first get a good understanding of the whole picture of that book or chapter. It's very simple for someone to take a Scripture out of its context in order to make their doctrines, their opinions, or their traditions seem right. That is a huge reason for all of the false teaching going on in the world today. That's why God wants us to know His entire Word.

It's important to remember that God looks at our heart. I've seen many Christians that could quote scriptures till the cows come home, but the wholeness of the Word doesn't abide in their heart. There's a huge difference between knowing God's Word and memorizing scriptures by the King James Version, New Living Version, New International Version, and so on. If you only know the red and the yellow, then you will never have a complete understanding of the color orange. I'm not at all suggesting that it's wrong to know a lot of verses by heart. I'm stressing the point of studying the wholeness of the Bible before you try to memorize individual pieces.

III. Examples Often Used

Now that I've explained what singling out scriptures is, let's look at some examples of it. As we go through some examples, try to see how easy it would be to believe in a certain doctrine just because it's in one part of the Bible. This is where your educated spiritual leaders can be a huge factor in your faith. Let them help you to see the whole picture and not just an incomplete Scripture that distorts the wholeness of the Bible.

a. Forbidden Meats

One good example of singling out scriptures is when people claim that we're not supposed to eat certain meats because the Bible tells us so in the Old Testament Law (Lev. 11). In the New Testament, which is the covenant we live under now, Paul tells us in 1st Timothy 4:4–5, *"For every creature of God is good, and nothing is to be refused if it is received with thanksgiving; for it is sanctified by the Word of God and prayer."* So basically, any food is clean as long as we give thanks to God and ask His blessing. Still, if someone is weaker in faith and feels like it is a sin to eat meat, then to them, it is sin (Rom. 14:1–3). This is one method that people use to try to prove their incomplete doctrines. They quote certain scriptures from the Old Testament that were later fulfilled and ultimately changed by Christ in the New Testament. Since these people don't use the whole Bible like they're supposed to, they can't find the whole truth. This is the reason why I always encourage newer Christians to get a solid understanding of the New Testament before they get into the Old Testament. There were many laws in the old covenant that were made obsolete by the new covenant with Jesus (Heb. 8:13). On the other hand, there are many of those old laws that Jesus still commands us to abide in. This is why the teachings of Jesus and those of the New Testament authors are so important to study on a regular basis. It keeps the devil from bringing confusion, which can ultimately lead to division.

Division is so dangerous because it gives the devil and all his evil forces a chance to work on believers in smaller groups. One large group of one hundred will be stronger than ten groups of ten. A good illustration of this would be a rope. A single strand of string can be easily pulled apart and snapped. But if you unite many strings together, you will have a solid and nearly unbreakable rope. That is why we as the whole church need to come together and form that solid rope.

b. What Defiles The Body?

I've often heard many people rightly say that, "...*your body is the Temple of the Holy Spirit*..." (1st Cor. 6:19) and you're not supposed to defile it. But then they add their own explanation of what does defile our body, not Jesus' explanation. The unlearned Christian will be quick to tell you that tattoos, piercings, certain meats, a crazy-colored hairdo, a glass of wine, or even baggy clothes are sinful because they defile your body (or your Temple). The problem with that is the fact that Jesus gives us a different explanation of what defiles our body. He tells us in Matthew 15:11 that it is "*Not what goes into the mouth defiles a man; but what comes out of the mouth, this defiles a man.*" And verse 18 says, "*...those things which proceed out of the mouth come from the heart, and they defile a man.*" Defilement does not come from anything we put in or on our physical bodies; it comes from the heart. You can "spiritually" defile yourself, but you can't "physically" defile your body. It has already been physically defiled from the original sin of Adam. No water baptism or sinner's prayer will ever remove the original sin from our body. These bodies of ours will one day go back to the dirt from which they came (Gen. 3:19). This is the reason why we need to be born again by the Spirit, because our physical bodies will never be acceptable enough to be with the Lord the way they are now (1st Cor. 15:50). As far as defilement goes, Jesus is telling us that from our heart (or spiritually) we make bad choices that defile ourselves. For example, overeating can defile you, not from the extra weight you put on your body, but from the gluttony that comes from your heart. It is the lack of self-control that causes you to sin, not the actual symptoms of it.

Murder is a physical act, but the act of killing itself isn't what defiles your body. The defilement comes from the choice that was made out of your heart to murder. In God's eyes, to truly hate someone to the point that you would kill them if you could get away with it is the same as murder (Matt. 5:21–22). This is because God sees our intentions whether we act on them or not. Alcohol or tobacco consumption is not what defiles our body. It is the addiction of these substances that comes from our heart and defiles us. Again, it is our lack of self-control and our dependence on these that cause addictions. We defile our Temples when our heart chooses to do wicked things, like those that are listed in Matthew 15:18–19. This is also why Jesus says in Matthew 5:28, "*But I say to you that whoever looks at a woman to lust for her has already committed adultery with her in his heart.*" As God's children, He knows our thoughts even before they manifest physically, and even if they never do. Isn't it sad to see men and women alike who don't mind if their spouse "looks at the menu as long as they don't order"? What I mean is that in many relationships, it is acceptable to gawk at the opposite sex, as long as they don't physically have any contact with them. If "look but don't touch" is the rule in your marriage, then you're saying that it's alright to cheat on God and defile your body spiritually, just so you don't cheat on your spouse physically.

God knows us by our Spirit, not by our defiled physical bodies. Since He can see the sin before it ever manifests physically, then we may not even go through with the sin according to man's terms, but we still may be charged with it in God's eyes. The motive behind the action is what God sees. In short, we should be striving to be pure inside and outside. Otherwise, we are nothing more than lukewarm Christians that are more interested in impressing people than God.

People have taken what defiles the body so far out of context that it has led to a physical, civil war between Christians instead of a spiritual war between good and evil. I am so thankful that God's my Judge and not a lot of the churches I've seen. It's sad to see Christians try to set their own standards for what a believer ought to be and not look to God's standards. It's as though some sins are accepted in the church, but there are other sins that immediately put the "*Not a Good Christian Yet*" label on you. Many Christians really seem to look down on other believers for smoking, drinking, listening to secular music, and for not being clean-cut. I'm not saying that all those things are good, but I do wonder how long it has been since these prejudging Christians went out witnessing to *unbelievers* instead of criticizing the ones who already believe in Christ. It's our job to tell people about Christ. The Holy Spirit will convict their hearts on the gray areas. I think that these pre-judgers forget about things like being overeating gluttons. Something occurred to me one day (while I was stuffing my face): Which one is better; having an overeating Christian who has little self-control, a Christian with a gambling problem, or one who smokes cigarettes? According to the Bible, there's no difference. One is addicted to snacking, the other to gambling, and the other is addicted to cigarettes. All three are dependant on their vises without self-control, but for some reason, many believers think that you can be a "Spirit filled Christian" if you're gluttonous, but not if you smoke or gamble. Who are we to say that one addiction is worse than the other? I'm certainly not encouraging smoking and gambling, but I am trying to show how the church labels equal sins so differently.

I've often noticed Christians rebuking other Christians for listening to secular music, even though they themselves watch secular TV shows and movies. Is it alright to hear secular talk on the television as long as it's not being sung on the radio? I'm not saying that any of it is *of God*, but we have to be careful not to be hypocritical in our judgment of others. That is something that unbelievers pick up on very quickly, and it gives them even more of a reason not to go to church. The things of the world are just something we're going to have to deal with. The most important thing we can do is love others unconditionally and not get too caught up in legalism. In Jesus' day, the Jews would walk right over sick and starving people so they could get to the Temple and make their sacrifices. Jesus wants us to love and care more about the needs of others rather than practicing religious traditions. For the Pharisees, the Law got so intertwined in their mind that they forgot the most important aspect of godliness—love. Someone once said that true happiness comes when your inner character (which is what God really knows us by) matches up with our outer person. If there is a large gap between the two, then the most you could ever hope for is a false sense of happiness. I believe it was this very point that James was making when he said, "*...faith without works is dead...*" (James 2:20). We show our faith in Christ by our love for other people, not necessarily by the "religious" things we do.

Today, we see the same mentality in legalistic believers everywhere. I wonder if these same people look at beautiful women or handsome men in a lustful way. Is it acceptable to sin in secret as long as you have the appearance of a Christian in public? This kind of singled-out faith is no different than the faith of the Pharisees. When you put laws, Christian traditions, or your personal appearance above love, then you become just like them.

Today, more than ever, we need to remove the plank from our own eye before we remove the speck out of our brother's eye (Matt. 7:5). A big misconception in the church today is that people have to be clean-cut and dress sharp in order to properly "reverence" the Lord. Reverence does not come from our physical appearance, it comes from our heart. I wonder if Jesus' appearance would be accepted in many of the churches today with the long hair and beard, robe and sandals. In the past few years of witnessing, I've seen one sad truth that keeps repeating itself: Satan will accept you no matter what you look like, but many churches will not. Some of the most on-fire Christians I've ever met had tattoos, face piercings, crazy dyed hair, and wild clothes. We need to understand that we can't identify a believer or an unbeliever just from their physical appearance, and not always by every action they do, either. Yes, Matthew 7:16 says, *"You will know them by their fruits . . ."* but we still need to look at their heart the way God looks at their heart. 1st Samuel 16:7 says, *". . . For the Lord does not see as man sees; for man looks at the outward appearance, but the Lord looks at the heart."* Jesus tells us again in John 7:24, *"Do not judge according to appearance, but judge with righteous judgment."*

Only God knows what we've all been through in the past, and that's how we are appreciated (Prov. 24:12). Not to mention the fact that God says He won't put on us any more than we can bear. This means that in some cases, God may decide to remove alcoholism from a new Christian's life before He works on their swearing. Maybe God is more concerned with helping a new Christian fight a bad drug habit than He is with getting that person to tithe in the church. God does give us the strength and the convictions to overcome the obstacles that are in our way, but He does it His way because only He knows exactly how much we can handle at one given time. The order in which *we* overcame worldly temptations may not be the same order everyone else has to follow. We're not going to be judged on a curve according to everyone else's experiences. We're going to be judged according to our own individual actions. There seems to be way too much condemning in the church and not enough love. We're probably guilty in one way or another of the same condemnations that we bring upon others. We certainly should offer our help and scriptural advice when we see our brothers and sisters falling off of God's path, but we should never do it in a way that we make ourselves look greater than them. This attitude makes us an offense to them, and anything you say will probably do more harm than good. It is important to practice this here on earth so we aren't so shocked when we get to Heaven and look at our actions through God's eye view. We need to remind ourselves that salvation isn't something you do or don't do. It is something you either believe in or don't.

c. Are we only supposed to pray to the Father, and not to Jesus?

Another dividing factor that has crept into the church is the notion that our prayers are only supposed to be directed to God the Father. This singled out teaching comes mainly from the Lord's Prayer that is spoken by Jesus in Matthew 6:9–13. Here, as He instructs His listeners how to pray, Jesus starts the prayer by saying, "*Our Father in heaven . . .*" This would certainly indicate that all prayers should be directed to the Father only, especially since Christ Himself told the people to pray that way. But before we let that single part of Scripture make our conclusion for us, we have to do a lot more searching.

In order to find the complete truth, we need to first start by understanding the person that Jesus was while He was on the earth. He was just as human as you and I are. This all-powerful, all-knowing, and omnipresent Son of God, who was the Creator from the beginning of time, just laid all of that glory aside so He could fulfill God's plan to save us. It's important to know that Jesus was *not* all-powerful in human form like He was in Heaven. He even told us that He had to rely on His Father for His strength and power. In John 5:30, Jesus said, "*I can of myself do nothing. As I hear, I judge;*

and my judgment is righteous, because I do not seek my own will but the will of the Father who sent Me." In the Garden of Gethsemane, Jesus was so emotionally stressed that He asked His Father if it was possible (and if it was His will) to take the suffering from Him (Matt. 26:39). There's no question that Jesus was powerful as a human being. However, He was not all-powerful like He was before and after His earthly life. His earthly power was given to Him by His Father according to His (the Father's) will. In John 3:27, we see that, *"...A man can receive nothing unless it has been given to him from heaven."* Jesus was under submission to His Father in Heaven. Scripture is clear that Jesus could have called upon the Father to save Him from death (Matt. 26:53), yet He chose to obey and stay on course for God's plan of salvation. Jesus willingly came to earth to suffer in place of us, but in doing so, He had to totally rely on His Father.

Jesus tells us in John 14:28 that the Father is greater than He is. This is because of the weaker incarnate state that Christ was in. Jesus had to lower Himself in order to be in the presence of sinful man. If you believe that Jesus is still a lesser deity than the Father now in Heaven, then you must deny the operation of the triune godhead called the Trinity. This was clearly a statement made only for Jesus' earthly years.

Jesus reveals to us in His Word that He was not all-knowing during His human years like He was in Heaven. This has been a big misunderstanding that many believers have taught over the years. Luke 2:52 tells us that, *"...Jesus **increased** in wisdom..."* This means that He had to learn just like we do. If He was all-knowing from the time He was conceived in Mary's womb until He grew up, then it would be impossible for Him to increase in wisdom. If He was always all-knowing, then we would have to assume that He spoke perfect Hebrew on the same day He was born. There are many places in the Bible where we see His human character. In Matthew 8:10, Jesus *"marveled"* at the Centurion for His great faith. This literally means that Jesus was amazed or surprised at the Centurion's act of faith. It would be difficult to be amazed or to marvel if you already knew the outcome.

In Mark 5:25–35, we read about a woman who had an issue of

blood for twelve years. She knew that if she could just touch Jesus' garment that she would be healed. When she touched Jesus' robe through the crowd, Jesus asked, "*Who touched My clothes?*" (verse 30). To say that it was rhetorical for Jesus to ask who touched Him doesn't make any sense. The only thing that the Bible says Jesus knew was that power had gone out of Him. The disciples obviously didn't view Jesus as being all-knowing because they responded by saying, "*. . . You see the multitude thronging You, and You say 'Who touched Me?'*" (verse 31). If the disciples thought Jesus knew everything, then they would have responded by saying, "Why would You ask a question that You already know the answer to?"

There were also dozens of other questions that Jesus asked throughout the Gospels. It would be false teaching for us to respond to *all* of them by saying, "He already knew every answer to those questions. He was just testing them." Like I said before, Jesus doesn't need us to twist the Bible around to make Him look greater. We need to keep His Word unchanged in order to get the clear picture of who He is. It's important to our faith to know that Christ was our perfect example of a human being. Otherwise, it wouldn't be fair for God to expect us to follow someone who couldn't relate to our weaknesses. You might ask, "If this is true, then how did Jesus know to tell Peter to get the temple tax out of the fish's mouth for Himself and Peter (Matt. 17:24–27)? How did Jesus foresee many of the events in His earthly life if He was not all-knowing?" The answer is through the miraculous gifts of the Holy Spirit. Jesus exercised these gifts on a regular basis. The lack of sin in His life made it easy for Him to use these gifts at will. You and I have these same opportunities as Christ had, but it is up to us as to how much sin we have separating us from God. He promises us in John 14:12 that we will be able to do the same works that He did, and even greater works because He will be able to empower us with the Holy Spirit once He's back in Heaven. Since none of us on earth is all-knowing, then Jesus must not have been, either. Otherwise, we would not be able to do the same works as He did, and this would have been an untruth told by Jesus. As Bible believing Christians, we should believe the author when he tells us in Hebrews 4:15, "*For we do not have a High*

Priest (Jesus) *who cannot sympathize with our weaknesses, but was in all points tempted as we are, yet without sin."* If we believe that Jesus had the same abilities on earth as He did and does now in Heaven, then it degrades who our God really is today.

The biggest reason for this belief is because some misinterpret the passage in Hebrews 13:8, saying, *"Jesus Christ is the same yesterday, today, and forever."* This book of Hebrews was written many years after Jesus died and was resurrected. So when this author said "yesterday," he was correct. He didn't say "Jesus is the same *when He was on earth*, today and forever." "Yesterday" could not have included His earthly life because it would degrade who He is today if we thought He was still the same. The point of that passage was to show that the Gospel of Christ was here to stay forever. We read in Hebrews 2:9 that Jesus was made a little lower than the angels. If we accept that Jesus was the same in his earthly life as He is today and forevermore, then we have to assume that He is *still* a little lower than the angels.

In order to settle any doubt of Jesus' earthly human side, I'm going to give you a perfect example from His own lips. In regard to His own return in Mark 13:32, Jesus tells us, *"But of that day and hour no one knows, not even the angels in Heaven,* **nor the Son***, but only the Father."* It would be a contradiction of Jesus' own words to say that He was all-knowing in His incarnate human state. He really didn't know when He was going to come back for His church because He didn't have the same abilities on earth as He does now from Heaven. Now He's back to His all-powerful, all-knowing, and omni-present self, like He was when He created this earth. So now we can safely say that He *does* know when He's going to return for us; He just didn't know at that time because He was subjected to human weaknesses just like we are and yet came out flawless. That's why He can relate to us on a personal level like no one else. That's why we know He would never fail us—because He already passed every test.

So we've seen how Christ couldn't have been all-powerful and all-knowing in His incarnate state, but what about Him being omni-present? I don't think this needs too much explaining. Just the fact that He was in bodily, human form should be enough to tell us that

He was only in one place at a time. Now from Heaven, He works as a part of an all-seeing and omnipresent godhead. Jesus even told us in John 14:12 that we will be able to do the same miracles as He did and more of them because He's going back to His Father. The reason for this is that He could work through each one of us as an empowered believer because of His omni-present ability from Heaven. This is an ability that He was unable to perform as a human. If Jesus was all-powerful, all-knowing, and omnipresent on earth, and if "we are able to do the same works that He did," then wouldn't that mean we're just like God? The Bible gives us a solid understanding of how Christ had to lower Himself from His true godly state.

Having said all of that, let's go back to the Lord's Prayer. Jesus told His disciples to pray to the Father because that's what He had to do. Since His resurrection, there's no reason in the Bible to believe that we can't pray directly to Jesus, or to the Holy Spirit, for that matter. In fact, Philippians 2:5–11 tells us that Christ, who was equal to God, came to the earth as a humble and obedient bondservant. After overcoming the death of the cross, God exalted Him and gave Him the name above every name. It goes on to say that everyone in Heaven, everyone on earth, and even everyone under the earth will one day bow and confess that this man, Jesus, is Lord. In the book of Acts, we see Peter praying in the name of Jesus (Acts 3:6) and even telling the new converts to be baptized in the name of Jesus (Acts 2:38). In the Gospels, Jesus never told anyone not to worship Him, nor did He ever deny His own deity. When you understand how this three-part godhead functions equally, then you'll see why we must accept all three. It's not enough to accept the Father but not the Son (John 3:35–36). This couldn't be said about an angel or any other power. Since that's what God's Word tells us, then we shouldn't have any reason why we can't pray to Jesus. The main issue here is that our prayers and our worship are glorifying God, no matter if it's through the Son or the Holy Spirit.

d. Should everything in our life be perfect once we're born again?

In this age of "name it and claim it" doctrines, a few scriptures have been singled out causing fallacies and discouragement from especially newer Christians. One Bible verse in particular that causes this incomplete doctrine by being singled out is Matthew 21:22. It says, *"And whatever things you ask in prayer, believing, you will receive."* The problem comes when we are taught that once we're saved, then we should be millionaires who never get sick as long as we pray for that *in faith.* The discouragement comes, obviously, when this doesn't happen. The best way I can direct someone in this case is to say that God never promised us a perfect life, but He does promise us a perfect afterlife. In our earthly life, God does have pleasure in seeing His children prospering, but He loves us enough to make sure we don't get spoiled, either. If we never went through trials, then we wouldn't appreciate the good times as much. If we never got a cold, then we wouldn't appreciate good health as much. If serving God meant a perfect earthly life, then it certainly wouldn't be the narrow way that few will find (Matt. 7:13–14). Every person in the world would serve God if it meant never being sick again or never having money problems. The truth is that Jesus doesn't want us to accept Him for what He can give us. He wants us to accept Him for what He's already given us. He's given us a chance to spend eternity in Heaven with Him and all of our saved loved ones. With this in mind, it's more important to Him that we spend eternity with Him rather than letting the pleasures of the world come between us and God. God will only give us as many blessings as we can handle before we start being ungrateful and putting things before Him. That's the responsibility of any father, and He's the greatest Father of all time.

What it all comes down to is putting things of this world before God. God needs to be *first* in our lives if we expect His perfect will to be done. Think of God as your umbrella (a really, really awesome umbrella). If everything in your life is under this umbrella and nothing is above it, then we can rest assured that God will take care of us in every way. Not according to our standards or the world's standards, but according to God's. But if you take something from your life and put it above your umbrella, then you're telling God that you will be responsible for that item. You're saying that you want to be in complete control of whatever it is. For example, if that item is your finances and you take it out of your umbrella (which is the covering of our Heavenly Father), then you can't expect God to be your provider. A sad reality of this is the fact that a very small percentage of born again believers actually give back to God a tenth (tithe) of what God has given them like He tells us to in Leviticus 26:30 and in Malachi 3:8–10. If God was really in control of your money, then your faith would be evident by your tithe. Another example is when we love our kids more than God so we put them above Him and outside of our umbrella. If we do this, then we can't expect God to protect them when we can't. We can't expect God to take care of their health or to keep them safe because we're kind of telling God "I'll take care of them." When we put anything above God, we do two things. First, we break the first and the most important commandment which is "*You shall have no other gods before Me.*" (Ex. 20:3). Yes, you yourself, a spouse, money, your children, addictions, and so on can be a god to us. This in itself should be more than enough reason to keep God first. Second, we take the bat out of the hands of the only Person who knows our needs more than we do ourselves. We kind of bite the hand that feeds us. Why wouldn't we let God be in charge of our health? He doesn't practice medicine, He perfected it. Why wouldn't we let God be in charge of our safety and the safety of our loved ones? He kept Shadrach, Meshach and Abed-Nego safe in a blazing, fiery furnace because they wouldn't put a false god before their God (Dan. 3:8–25). Why wouldn't we trust God to provide for us and our family? He owns the entire world and every creature in it. In Psalms 50:10–12, God tells us, "*For every beast of the forest is Mine, And the cattle on a thousand hills. I know all the birds of the mountains, And the wild beasts of the field are Mine… For the world is Mine, and all its fullness.*"

This doesn't mean that ungodly people will never be rich or healthy. Nor does it mean that a righteous person will never be sick, poor, or even hungry. I'm just saying that if every aspect of your life is under the covering of Almighty God, then our joys become His joys.

Our problems become His problems. Our bills become His bills. Our pain becomes His pain. Our children, and spouse, and ourselves become God's sheep with Jesus Christ as our Shepherd. When God is above everything to you, then He will be glorified through your life. When you truly are in love with Jesus on a personal level, you won't be as concerned with all the blessings that He can give you. You will be more concerned with what you can do for Him. In this age of "name it and claim it," the most important thing we should claim is Jesus Christ as our Lord and Savior and our desire to see only His will done in our lives. When we do this, God will meet our needs. Not all of our wants, but all of our needs.

I could go on forever listing examples of how Bible verses have been butchered by being singled out. I'm hoping that you can see how to identify them and learn to keep them in their proper place. If you can do this, then you can be sure that you're following God's Word and not substituting orange for red and yellow. You should always be cautious of a church or a belief that is founded on one or two Bible verses. Search it out for yourself and find God's answer.

The Bible Formula 6

So far we've looked at God's plan of salvation and why we need Jesus. We've identified "overshooting" and its consequences. And we just looked at how singling out scriptures can lead to false teaching. The main target of this book is to remove human error from our many different beliefs in an attempt to find the truth. Truth is what we need to reach the unbelievers in the world because they can usually tell when something is not genuine. In this chapter, I want to explain how we can use the Bible to establish different truths that we can have solid faith in, not because we we're taught them by man, but because we have seen them for ourselves in the Word of God. Remember, at your judgment you're not going to be judged according to the teachings and traditions of your teachers. You will be judged according to the Word of God.

As I have said before, having an open mind is the key to finding the truth. You must be willing to swallow your pride and accept that you might have been taught certain things the wrong way. Don't assume that you *have* been taught incorrectly. Just know the possibility is there. Not only is this a humbling experience, but it also allows you to have more faith in your beliefs once you let the Bible, instead of man, prove them for you.

There is a way that we can find many more truths and bring an end to so many of these church denominations. These churches are separated by different beliefs. Some are small differences, and others are much greater. So let's stop trying to find the Pentecostal way, or the Baptist way, or the Catholic way, and let's try to find God's way.

I. How the Formula Works

We can solve Bible differences by using what I call "The Bible Formula." What you do is take a particular belief or doctrine that has been the subject of debate. You take all of the scriptures from all sides of the argument that pertain to that doctrine without taking them out of their original context. Once you put them all together, you will hopefully end up with only one possible answer that will satisfy all of those scriptures. If you were taught to believe one certain way, then you probably already know all the scriptures that support that side of the debate. If you want to find the complete truth, then it is up to you to find all of the scriptures that seem to support the other side(s) of the debate as well. Find someone who believes the opposite of you about a certain doctrine and get all of their supporting scriptures for that belief. Maybe he or she will sit down with you and go through this formula with you.

We, as Christians, should believe that the Bible is the inspired Word of God. That means even though it was written by human beings, God was in complete control of its authorship (2nd Tim. 3:16). If we accept that every Word in the Bible is true, then we must also accept that there are no contradictions. We must understand that even if there seems to be parts of the Bible that contradict one another, there must be an explanation for it. This explanation has to include all sides of the argument in order for us to accept that the whole Bible is true. If we accept one side of the argument and not the scriptures that support the other side of the argument, then we are taking away from the Bible to form our own doctrine. By doing this, we're basically saying that the scriptures that support the other side of the debate are not important or may even be incorrect. What you end up with is only a portion of the truth. To find the whole truth about a certain Bible belief, we have to take *all* of the pertaining scriptures into account. Through prayer, godly wisdom, and common sense, you should come up with many more answers that fit the whole Bible without having to ignore other parts of the Bible or having to assume they are wrong.

II. Flexible Scriptures

Before we begin to plug different Bible doctrine into the Bible formula, we have to realize that some scriptures are "flexible." What this means is that if two or more scriptures that are used in their proper context seem to contradict each other, then at least one of them must bend (or be flexible) in order for us to continue our belief that every Word in the Bible is true. We cannot accept contradictions in the Bible, so we must use all pertaining scriptures in the original translation if necessary to find the truth, not just the ones we need to prove our own opinions.

It's important to know the difference between identifying a Scripture as being flexible and actually compromising that Scripture to try to make it into something that it's not. Jesus was referred to as the "Lamb of God," but that doesn't mean He was a four-legged animal covered in wool. Many times, the Bible uses links, analogies, parables, and different comparisons to get God's point across. We must learn when to dig deep word for word, and we must know when not to dig too far so that we go pass what God wants us to see. Sometimes statements are meant to be used in a broad and general manner, but others are for a very specific situation. Knowing which is which is the key to solving Bible mysteries and doctrines.

III. The Parable of The Block and The Shapes

I'll use a comparison to help you better understand what flexible scriptures are. When I was a kid, I remember playing with different plastic shapes. These shapes had to fit into a block that also had those same shapes cut in them. The square shape would only fit into the square cutout in the block. The circle shape would only fit into the circle cutout, and so on. Sometimes in the Bible, there may appear to be two or more verses that contradict each other.

a. The Angels At Jesus' Tomb

A quick example of this would be if you compare Luke 24:4 with Matthew 28:2-3. In Luke, he speaks of two angels being at the tomb of Jesus, whereas Matthew only records one angel being there. These two instances in the Bible could be compared to us trying to put the plastic square shape into the circle cutout. They may not fit together just right, but if you push hard enough, it will eventually go in. The reason that the square shape is able to go into the circle cutout is because either the plastic square shape bends (or flexes) to fit inside the cutout, or because the cutout expands (or flexes) to allow the square shape to fit. In some cases, both the plastic shape *and* the cutout must flex in order to make them fit together. When different parts of the Bible appear to contradict each other, we must accept that one or more of those scriptures are flexible. Otherwise, we have to accept that the Bible is wrong. In the case of the angels at Jesus' tomb, we must accept that there were at least two angels there, and that Matthew only saw one of them or that he only chose to write about one of them. This is not a contradiction because they were both right. There was one angel at the tomb, but there was also another one. If Matthew said, "There was one **and only one** angel at Jesus' tomb," then there would be a true contradiction. However, in this case they were both giving their own accounts of this point in history, and they both were correct. Remember, the Bible has proven itself to be accurate for thousands of years. There's no reason at all to believe there are any contradictions in it.

b. Will everyone die once?

Another good example of scriptures having to bend in order to find the truth begins in Hebrews 9:27. Here, the author tells us, "*... it is appointed for men to die once, but after this the judgment . . .*" This verse is basically saying that we will all die one time and then will be judged. If we compare that verse with 1st Corinthians 15:51 and 1st Thessalonians 4:15–17, then we can see another apparent contradiction. These two verses tell us that *not* everyone will die (sleep), but that some are just going to be changed instantly into an immortal body and then be caught up with the Lord in the air (raptured). By plugging these verses into the Bible formula, we have to allow at least one of these verses to flex. In this case, we can see that there must be some people who will never die because 1st Corinthians 15:51 comes right out and tells us this. Otherwise, this would be a lie in God's Word, and that is an unacceptable answer. So if we combine these two verses about not dying with the original Scripture in Hebrews 9:27, then we can see where the flexibility needs to be, and we can come up with a better understanding about death. That truth is that everyone who is not raptured will die once. Wasn't that easy? The point that the author was trying to make in that part of the book of Hebrews wasn't that we all *had* to die once. The point was that just as we die once and then we are judged, so also did Jesus have to die once to bear the sins for our judgment. It was a very general statement, so it must be used in a general matter and not as a specific point. The Holy Spirit will help you understand this better as you ask for guidance. This example is another reason why you cannot single out scriptures in the Bible.

c. Are all sins equal?

Sometimes people feel like they couldn't possibly serve the Lord because they know they are going to continue to sin. They believe that even tiny mistakes are just as bad in God's eyes as large sins. Basically, *sin is sin*! Well, this is somewhat true, but mostly deceiving. You can see where this belief comes from when you read James 2:10. Here it says, *"For whoever shall keep the whole law, and yet stumble in one point, he is guilty of all."* James is not telling us that it's just as bad to swear when you stub your toe as it is to rape somebody. He's not saying that arguing with your parents is as bad of a sin as murder.

Let's continue looking in God's Word because with all doctrines, we must look at other pertaining scriptures in order to find the whole truth. In Ezekiel, we read a totally different side of this question. In chapter 16, he warns Jerusalem that they have become more wicked than even the pagan cities. He tells them in Ezekiel 16:52 that, *"... the sins which you committed were **more abominable** than theirs; they are more righteous than you . . ."* God comes right out and says that some sins are worse than others. There should be no misunderstanding of that.

What we need to do in order to find the one and only truth that will satisfy the entire Bible is to identify which of these scriptures can flex. Obviously, they both have to be right; otherwise, the Bible wouldn't be infallible. Both of these scriptures are, in fact, correct when you plug them into the rest of God's Word. Sometimes there *is* no difference in sin. Sin is what separates us from God, no matter how great or small it is. Look at how Adam and Eve caused The Fall of Man in the first place just by eating something they weren't supposed to. I'll bet most of us are guilty of this everyday. Lucifer's sin that kicked him out of heaven was pride and covetousness to be like God. This wasn't a malicious sin, yet it was enough to separate him from God. Sins are equal in that they all should be confessed and asked for forgiveness, regardless of the nature or size of the sin.

So sins are equal in some ways, but they certainly are not the same in other respects. The Bible tells in Matthew 12:31 that blasphemy of the Holy Spirit is an unpardonable sin that cannot be forgiven. If blasphemy of the Holy Spirit is unforgivable and all sins were the same, then no sins could be washed away by the blood of Jesus. We know that the Bible doesn't teach this. The only reason Christ died for us is so we can be forgiven and found clean in God's eyes. In the Old Testament, different sins carried with them different punishments. Small crimes were treated with small consequences, and heinous crimes received very harsh punishments. This is a part of the old law that must still exist today so that we can always strive to serve God better. It gives us an opportunity to rate our progress and growth with the Lord. Paul backs up this statement concerning the old law when he says in Romans 7:4, "... *I would not have known sin except through the law* ... " The law not only shows us what sin is, but it also shows us what sins are considered worse by the punishment that was given. If you only read James 2:10, then you would believe that there is no difference in sins. You must never be satisfied with an entire doctrine by reading one Bible passage. There's usually more somewhere else to go along with it. In Matthew 18:16, Jesus tells us "... *by the mouth of two or three witnesses every word may be established.*" We need to use this concept when finding Bible doctrines.

When you understand the context that scriptures are to be used in, then you can understand which scriptures can flex and which ones cannot. That is what the Bible formula really is; using all of the scriptures that pertain to a certain subject in their proper context without overshooting. When God tells us "Thou shall not kill," then common sense should tell us that He is referring to murder. Otherwise, it would be a contradiction of His own Word when God commanded the sacrifice of certain animals in the old Law or when He led the Israelites into war. If this commandment was not flexible, then we wouldn't even be able to eat fruits and vegetables because we couldn't kill the living plants. When Christians can't discern whether or not scriptures are flexible, then the devil has a perfect opportunity to divide us through false teachings. If we could study and search and swallow our pride about who's right or wrong, then we as Bible believers could agree on more things. We would stop dividing our church.

The point is that if you truly believe every word in the Bible, then you can use this formula to find the truth about the different doctrines that has separated churches for so long. Don't accept or just ignore apparent contradictions in God's Word. Let the Bible prove itself. Don't settle for an incomplete doctrine when you know there is Scripture that goes against what you believe. Keep in mind that Satan uses half truths to lure people to him. Don't put yourself in his class by doing the same thing.

Sometimes Bible mysteries are as easy to solve as putting the circle shape into the circle cutout. However, sometimes God wants us to search out different matters and do a little bit of studying for His sake. 2nd Timothy 2:15 tells us to, *"Be diligent to present yourself approved to God, a worker who does not need to be ashamed, rightly dividing the word of truth."* Proverbs 25:2 tells us that, *"It is the glory of God to **conceal** a matter, But the glory of kings is to **search out** a matter."* The reason for the hidden mysteries is because God is looking for a remnant of people who will thirst after His righteousness. He's looking for the ones who are willing to work for Him and not be lazy. It is this very remnant of believers that Jesus can use mightily on earth and in Heaven. This is where we as Christians can be set apart for His glory.

Don't make the mistake of thinking that it's not your job to search out the Bible. Don't think that you can lean solely on your pastor's word and not God's Word, too. Any honest pastor will tell you that they don't know everything. They still make many mistakes.

The only perfect example that you'll ever find is Jesus Christ and His Word. Just as this book can be used as a guide to help build your faith, it is certainly no substitute for the Bible. It is crucial that we all understand the importance and the infallibility of God's Word.

This formula will show you answers that may change your life and certainly may change your beliefs. It will also change your level of faith because all of your beliefs will come from the infallible Word of God instead of man. Imagine if you were a builder and the soon-to-be homeowner gave you the exact measurements for building his new house. Let's say that if the house was not built exactly according to his specs, then you would have all of eternity to pay for your errors. Would you just trust your crew to build it exactly right, or would you want to at least check it for yourself to *know* that it's being built according to the measurements given to you by the owner? I'm sure you would want to check it, especially since you are the one who is going to be held accountable for the accuracy of the home.

This is obviously an exaggerated story, but the principle is the same for our lives as Christians. The reason for this demonstration is to show you two things. First, it is crucial for us to search out the Bible on our own and be open-minded to it. This is especially true since we will be accountable for our own actions on our judgment day (2nd Cor. 5:10). Second, as long as we follow the measurements (the Bible) that our Boss (God) has given us, then we know can know for sure that we're living a purposeful life. We don't have to worry if other people think the Bible has mistakes in it. What worldly people call mistakes might just be the way God wanted it to be. After all, He is the owner, and our purpose should be to see His will done—no one else's.

Putting It All Together 7

Part 1 Salvation And Accountability

Hopefully by now you're better educated on how to properly find the answers that the Bible gives us. God tells us in 2nd Peter 1:20 that, "*... no prophesy of Scripture is of any private interpretation ...*" Knowing this, we should seek out the one truth that God intends. So far, I've tried to show how we can find that truth by letting the Bible prove our doctrines and beliefs for us with less risk of letting in human error. Now we're going to put all of the teachings from the previous chapters together and see how we can come up with the correct answers for a few different Bible beliefs. We're going to go through some examples of the different doctrines that have split up churches in the past, and we're going to try to find God's answer for them. Please keep in mind that if you're convinced that your belief has been proven to be wrong, then that doesn't make you a bad person. However, if you continue to believe and teach false doctrines after the Bible has shown you the truth, then there will be a great accountability on your day of judgment. It's not anyone's opinion that matters; it's only what the Bible says. It's my prayer that even if you're not convinced of the following doctrines, then you will at least dig in deeper to find more answers.

I. Can we fall from god's grace, or once saved, always saved?

The first church-dividing argument that we're going to look at is whether or not you can backslide and go to hell once you've been born again. Some Christians believe that if you've accepted Christ as your Lord and Savior and then you lose your faith in Christ and go back to your sinful life, then you were never really born again to begin with. These ones believe that once you're saved, you're always saved because you can never lose your salvation. The other side of the debate is that you can truly be saved and then fall from God's grace because of your own free will choice to deny your faith in Christ. Both sides of this argument have significant Scripture references to support their belief of this topic. We're going to try to use these scriptures to come up with one complete truth to satisfy this debate.

a. Falling From Grace

We will begin by looking at the scriptures that support the belief of "falling from grace" once you've been born again. As we list each supporting Scripture, we have to make sure that they're being used in the right context of the Bible. We also have to watch out for overshooting and flexibility. Instead of twisting them to find the view that we want, we must use these scriptures the way God intended them to be used so we can find the truth.

I will list and explain each pertaining Scripture, starting from the front of the Bible and working my way to the back. The first part of the Bible we will look in is Ezekiel 18:19–32. Here, the prophet Ezekiel begins by explaining to the Israelites that they have their own choice whether or not to be righteous, regardless of their fathers' actions. In verse 21, Ezekiel tells the people that if a wicked man turns from his sins (repents) and does what is lawful and right, then there will be eternal life for him. It would be as though he was never wicked in the first place (v. 22). In verse 24, Ezekiel contrasts this point by claiming that if a righteous man turns *away* from his righteousness and becomes like the wicked man, then he will die and he will not have eternal life. This would be as though the man were never righteous in the first place.

Ezekiel makes an even stronger case for this belief in chapter 33. In the 12th verse if this chapter, God comes right out and tells Ezekiel to warn the people that, "*... the righteousness of a righteous man **will not deliver him** ...*" if he rebels (transgresses) from it. Again in verse 18 of the 33rd chapter, he is told by God to warn Israel that, "*When a righteous man **turns** from his righteousness and commits iniquity, he shall die because of it.*" This is a very compelling point that cannot be re-written, ignored, or changed. The word "righteous" comes from the Hebrew word "*tsaddiq,*" which means one who is right, just, clear, clean, or justified. Before Jesus came to earth, people were justified through the Law of Moses. Now we're justified and ultimately saved through our faith in Christ. This word clearly could apply to someone who was in God's grace. Even though the examples in Ezekiel don't refer to born again believers (because Christ had not yet come), Ezekiel could be speaking of somebody who could fall from God's grace.

In the 10th chapter of Matthew, Jesus commissioned the twelve disciples to go and spread the Gospel. In verse 22, Jesus tells them, "*And you will be hated by all for my sake. But he who endures **to the end** will be saved.*" This verse implies that one would not only have to be born again but remain born again until the end. According to this Scripture, enduring to the end is necessary for salvation.

Probably one of the more direct verses in the Bible that pertains to this belief of falling from grace is in Romans 11. Here, Paul is comparing backsliders (people who fall away from their godly ways) to a wild olive tree. Verse 20 tells us that some are like the branches of an olive tree that were once a part of the tree but now are broken off. In verse 23, Paul tells us, "*And they also, if they **do not continue in unbelief**, will be grafted in, for God is able to graft them in **again**.*" Paul is pretty straightforward here. He's basically saying that if we fall away from our faith but do not continue in our unbelief, then God will graft us in again. Right after that, in verse 25, it's interesting that Paul says, "*For I do not want you to be ignorant of this mystery lest you should be wise in your own opinion . . .*" It seems as though Paul wrote this part of Romans just for this reason, so there would be no argument or division on whether or not you can fall from grace.

In 1st Corinthians 15, Paul is teaching the church in Corinth about what the necessary belief is in order to be saved. In verse 1 and 2, he tells the people of Corinth that it is the Gospel of Jesus Christ "*by which also you are saved, **if** you hold fast that gospel that I preached to you . . .*" This means they will be saved *if* they continue to believe in Christ; otherwise, they will fall.

In the 5th chapter of James, there is an important point made as

James addresses how the churches should conduct themselves. In verses 19 and 20, James tells the people, "*Brethren, if anyone among you wanders **from the truth**, and someone **turns him back**, let him know that he who turns a sinner from the error of his way will **save a soul from death** . . .*" This statement gives us a clear picture of someone who is bound for Heaven, then falls from God's grace, then is able to be brought back and saved again from death. The phrase, "wanders from the truth" implies that the person at one time believed the truth. We know that Jesus Christ is the Way, the **Truth**, and the Life (John 14:6) James 5:20 claims that by turning that "one-time believer" back to the truth about Christ, you will save his soul from hell.

The last Scripture that I am going to use that supports the falling from grace belief is in the 3rd chapter of Revelation. The author, John, writes about the church of Sardis as it is revealed to him through a vision of Jesus. In verse 2–3, Jesus states that this church's works are becoming dead, and He tells them to hold fast and repent. In Revelation 3:5, Jesus says, "*He who overcomes shall be clothed in white garments, and **I will not blot out his name from the Book of Life**; but I will confess his name before My Father and before His angels.*" Whether or not Jesus is talking directly to you and me in these verses, one thing is for sure; He clearly is able to "blot your name out of the Book of Life." The only way He could blot your name out of Heaven's list is to have your name in the Book of Life in the first place. The only way your name could be in this Book is if you are born again (John 3:3). The phrase "he who overcomes shall be clothed in white" means that whoever repents and endures with Him to the end will be found righteous in God's sight. "Clothed in white garments" is an expression that Jesus equates with as being righteous (similar to a virgin wearing a white wedding dress). To sum this all up, Jesus is saying that if you stay righteous until the end, then your name will remain on the list of those people who will live with God forever.

These different Bible scriptures, when they are used in the right context, make a solid case that you certainly can fall from God's grace. In fact, if you don't believe that you can still go to hell once you've been born again and have backslidden, then you must assume that these scriptures are inaccurate. If you ignore or remove these parts of the Bible, then you've taken away from God's Word, and you may as well throw away the entire Bible. In Revelation 22:19, John gives everyone a firm warning not to add to or take away from God's Word or else He will add plagues and take away blessings.

Even though the Word appears to tell us that you are not out of the woods until you're feet hit them streets of gold, there is still the other side of the debate to study in order to reach the complete truth. I will list some scriptures that people use to support the "once saved, always saved" belief. Keep in mind the Bible formula as we plug the scriptures in to come up with hopefully one true answer.

Hebrews 6:4–6 is a part of the Bible that I have heard used for both sides of this argument. Here, the author tells us, *"For it is impossible for those who were once enlightened, and have tasted the heavenly gift, and have become partakers of the Holy Spirit, and have tasted the good Word of God and the powers of the age to come, if they fall away, to renew them again to repentance, since they crucify again for themselves the Son of God, and put Him to an open shame."* Without really looking into these verses, you might think that it supports the "once saved, always saved" belief. The truth is these verses actually prove that we can fall away from God's grace once we were really born again. The phrase "if they fall away" proves without a doubt that someone can fall away. Let me paraphrase these verses to make it easier to understand. "If you were saved once, and then you fall away, then it would be impossible to renew you again to repentance." We know that these ones who "fall away" must have been saved at one time, because you can't taste the heavenly gift or be a partaker of the Holy Spirit unless you're born again (1st Cor. 2:12, John 3:5). Romans 8:9 tells us *"... if anyone does not have the Spirit of Christ, he is not His."* The author makes sure to stress this point so there is no doubt that these are born again believers that have fallen away. I don't see how anyone who believes every word of the Bible can read this passage and still believe you can never fall away from the Lord once you were born again. This should not be a doctrine that splits up churches.

b. What does it mean to "renew them again to repentance"?

Now the question to ask shouldn't be "Can we fall from grace?" but "Can we be back in God's grace a second time once we were born again and then fell away?" In order to answer this, we need to understand what it means to "renew them again to repentance," then I'll come back to the scriptures that support the belief of "once saved, always saved." Hebrews 4:6 is often misinterpreted by surface readers. On the surface, this phrase would seem to say that it's impossible to repent and serve the Lord again once you've been saved and then have fallen away. If we look deeper into the Word, then we'll find the real answer. The following explanation is how I interpret the scriptures on this subject. The key words in verse 6 are "renew again to repentance." When you give your heart to the Lord, you must turn away from your sinful life (with the help of the Holy Spirit) and live a life of righteousness. This is called repentance. The author is saying that if you get saved and repent from your sinful ways, and then you fall away from your faith, then it's impossible for you to ever have that new original repentance again like the first time. The reason for this is that once you know right from wrong and you still choose to do wrong, then ignorance can't be an excuse anymore. The latter part of Hebrews 6:6 tells us that when we keep going back to our sinful ways, we put Jesus to an open shame. There is definitely going to be a consequence to pay. For example, God forgave the apostle Paul for murdering those Christians before he knew the Lord (Acts 9:21, 1st Tim. 1:13). If Paul would have later returned to that insolent life but then repented for a second time, then Hebrews 6:6 says that his slate wouldn't be wiped completely clean again like the first time because it would require Jesus to be crucified all over again. The word "renew" means to make new, just like its original state. When we sin willfully after we know right from wrong, then God will still forgive us (1st John 1:9). However, there will have to be a consequence since we can't use ignorance as an excuse. When we willfully *backslide*, knowing that it's wrong, then God *will* still take us back (Matt. 18:22). Jeremiah 3:14 says, *"Return, O backsliding children," says the Lord; "for I am married to you."* It just won't be the same as the original repentance where God "remembered your sin no more." Since it's impossible to return to new (or to have a perfectly clean slate again) if we fall from God's grace and then come back, then we have to accept that there will be a consequence for backsliding. 1st Corinthians 3:8–15 explains how we will first be judged according to our faith in Christ, and then according to our works on earth. If we continue to live a sinful life after we've accepted Jesus as our Lord and Savior, then one of two things will happen; either we won't make it into Heaven, or we will just barely make it in with little or no rewards to show for our labor on earth. This is compared in 1st Corinthians 3:15 as someone being *"... saved, yet so as through fire."*

If you're one of those people out there (like I used to be) who don't want to change your life just yet even though you know you should, then keep in mind that you're not being ignorant, you're being disobedient. That disobedience could be costing you rewards in Heaven (if you even make it). When you *know* you're not living the life that you should be living, then you're accountable for whether or not you repent. If you say that you don't want to get saved until you're ready to get your life straightened up first, then you're not helping yourself. God wants you the way that you are. Don't try to change your life without His help, because it won't work. Let the Holy Spirit change you. God's covenant with us gives us the opportunity to be completely forgiven of our sins. He even said that He would not remember our sinful past anymore once we come to know the Lord (Jer. 31:34). It is, however, up to us to live a life of Godliness from then on with the help of the Holy Spirit. If we show no spiritual growth, and continue in our sinful ways, then that's not truly repentance. Yes, we're all going to sin once and a while, but God judges us according to our faith in His Son and our *effort* to live a life of righteousness. That's not to say that there will be *no* consequence of our sins as we live for the Lord. If we can fight off the temptations of the devil, then our judgment will be prosperous not only for us, but for the ones whose lives we've touched also. 1st Timothy 6:12 tells us to *"Fight the good fight of faith, lay hold on eternal life..."* If you continue in sin with little or no sign of repentance, then you must question whether or not your faith in Christ is real.

If you truly believe that God is with us, and He sees all that you do, then your actions should change according to your belief.

It's important to understand what it means to "renew them again to repentance," but without getting anymore off track, let's look at some scripture references that support the belief of "once saved, always saved."

c. Once saved, always saved?

Many times, Christians who don't believe in being able to lose their salvation make the mistake of using themselves or a loved one as an example. They may think that Bob, Joe, or someone else they know (including themselves) never lost their faith, so it must not be possible. The question is not whether or not you or a loved one has lost their salvation. The question is not even if we can tell whether or not someone is saved. The question is whether or not it is *possible* to lose salvation once you've had it. To the people that truly have fallen off the spiritual wagon, it would be easy to say that they were never saved in the first place. And I tend to agree with this belief to a point because just as there are different levels of sin and wickedness, there are also different levels of faith. If you have a true, solid faith in Jesus, then there's probably nothing that will separate you from God. However, if you're weak in faith, you may still be on the road to Heaven, but you will be more susceptible to losing your faith because of worldly circumstances. A Christian who is weak in faith could be like one "... *saved, yet so as through fire.*" (1st Cor 3:15). Given the above scriptures about losing salvation, I believe the Bible is pretty clear that you can have a spiritual birth, and then, that same new life can later die off through a lack of belief and acceptance of Christ. If faith in Christ causes a new birth in you, couldn't you later deny Christ and say "good-bye" to the very life that was caused from believing? The Bible gives me a clear understanding that everything we have, including eternal life, comes with conditions that need to be met in order to be fulfilled. I don't think it's impossible for a weak Christian, like the ones described in 1st Corinthians 3:15, to later renounce Jesus. John 10:10 tells us, "*the thief does not come except to steal, and to kill, and to destroy.*" Satan certainly knows what buttons to push to try to get born again believers back to disbelief. And even though we may not be able to judge the hearts of people as to whether they have lost their faith or not, the issue is whether or not it's possible.

If you only looked at the scriptures that support this belief, then it would be very convincing and easy to think that way. Let's look at some scriptures that are used to support the "once saved-always saved" belief and combine them with the ones we've already looked at.

In the first chapter of Ephesians, Paul opens up his letter by praising God and by giving a brief explanation of Christ's reason for coming as our Savior. In Ephesians 1:13–14, Paul promises that if you have heard and believed in the Gospel of Jesus Christ then, "... *you were **sealed** with the Holy Spirit of promise, who is the guarantee of our inheritance until the redemption of the purchased possession ..."* This verse would appear to say that once you've believed in the Gospel of Jesus, then the Holy Spirit seals your salvation up until you die, and you can never lose it. Another similar Bible verse is Romans 11:29, where Paul tells us, *"For the gifts and the calling of God are **irrevocable**."* This verse could easily be misconstrued as "once saved-always saved" since salvation is a gift, and the gifts of God are irrevocable. Keep in mind that this verse says that the "calling" of God is irrevocable, too. In 1st Samuel 10, Saul was chosen or "called" to be the first king of Israel. 1st Samuel 13:13–14 tells us that before Saul's disobedience, *"... the Lord **would have** established your kingdom over Israel forever. But now your kingdom shall not continue. The Lord has sought for Himself a man after His own heart ..."* God took the calling that was on Saul's life and gave it to David. As I will explain in a moment, irrevocable is a flexible word that must be used in the proper context and must not contradict any other part in the Bible.

John 5:24 is another verse used to support *"once saved, always saved."* It tells us, *"Most assuredly, I say to you, he who hears My word and believes in Him who sent Me has everlasting life, and shall not come into judgment, but has passed from death into life."* This is definitely a true statement, but this only applies to someone who believes in Jesus. If the faith is later lost, then the new life dies with it. There's nothing in this verse that claims a faith in Christ can never be turned around. Again, if there were a verse that came out and said that you can not lose your salvation, then that would completely contradict other parts of the Bible (ex. Heb 6:4–6, James 5:19–20, etc.) That's why it's important to find which scriptures have the potential to flex, and which ones cannot.

Another scripture that supports this belief is John 10:28. Here, Jesus says *"And I give them eternal life, and they shall never perish; neither shall anyone snatch them out of my hand."* Eternal life in heaven isn't guaranteed until we actually get to heaven. At that time, we will certainly never perish. There is no doubt that your faith in Christ can never be taken (or snatched) away by anyone, but there's no reason here to believe that you yourself can't lose your faith. If faith in Christ is the very essence of a new life, then it stands to reason that a later denial of that faith can cause death.

In Ephesians 1:4–5, we see another part of scripture that has been used to support the belief of never being able to lose your salvation. Here, we read, *"just as He chose us in Him before the foundation of the world, that we should be holy and without blame before Him in love, having predestined us to adoption as sons by Jesus Christ to Himself, according to the good pleasure of His will."* It's important to realize that God has predestined **everyone** of us to live with Him in Heaven. Again, we read in 2nd Peter that the Lord is *"not willing that any should perish but that all should come to repentance."* God never chose or predestined anyone to go to hell. If He did, then you could definitely say that someone was once and always saved since God already would have had it all planned. But God allows our free will to determine our future, even when it means going against His perfect will. As I explained in the Free will part of chapter 2, I believe scripture shows that God doesn't choose to foresee every person's outcome for every situation. All of that makes Ephesians 1:4–5 irrelevant to this debate.

The last scripture I want to use to support the "once saved, always saved" belief is in 2nd Corinthians 5:17. Here, Paul tells us, *"Therefore, if anyone is in Christ, he is a new creation; old things have passed away; behold, all things have become new."* I can relate to this verse all too well. God changed my whole life. As long as I remain in Christ, I am a new creation. I remain in Him through my faith in Him and the remissions of my sins. This verse still doesn't promise that one can never fall from Christ. In all of my searching of this debate, God's Word stands without contradiction. It's difficult to see any way to reverse this doctrine and still be able to satisfy the entire Bible. We can only work with the parts of the Bible that can flex. Other parts are so cut and dry that they only appear to mean one thing.

If you just concentrated on these latter Bible verses, then I could see how it would be easy to think that it's impossible to lose your salvation. In fact, if it weren't for all of the opposing scriptures, then there would be a strong case for this belief. Unfortunately, instead of taking all of the above Bible verses, these verses have been singled out by many Christians to argue that it is impossible to lose your salvation. Those who teach this doctrine will often respond by saying that if a believer does fall away from their faith in Christ, then they were never really saved in the first place. That may be the case most of the time, but the Word is clear that you can lose your salvation. Knowing this, I would hope Christians took their spiritual journey more serious. I would hope that Christians wouldn't put all the trust of eternal security into this life, causing them to be slack in their faith. That is the real importance of this debate.

Allow me to continue to finish this debate. We already know from Hebrews 6:4–6, that you can be born again (by accepting Jesus as your Savior and partaking of the Holy Spirit) and then fall away. Since these verses seem to be a contradiction with the verses above that appear to support "once saved, always saved," then we have to assume that there is some flexibility somewhere. That's the key to solving Bible mysteries. As far as salvation goes, we have to realize that whatever God gives us comes with conditions. Adam and Eve had conditions in order to live forever in the Garden of Eden and had that privilege removed due to their actions.

Since we read in 1st Samuel 13:13–14 that King Saul's calling was removed because of his disobedience to God, then it makes sense that we can lose gifts and callings. We just need to know what Paul meant by "sealed" and "irrevocable."

Using previous examples in the Bible is a good way to tell how we as Bible studying Christians can identify which scriptures can flex and which ones can not. Between Saul losing his calling, and the fact that Hebrews 6:4–6 directly tells us that we can lose our salvation, then we must accept that "sealed" and "irrevocable" do not prove otherwise. If they did, then the Bible would be wrong with contradictions. And if you believe that one part of the Bible is wrong, then there's no sense in believing any of it. Don't make the stubborn mistake of just accepting one side of this debate and ignoring the other, even if you were taught this way your whole life. It should be more important as a Christian to offer a pure and accurate Word of God than to always have to be right about a doctrine. Not only does this belief divide churches, but it sends people to hell every day also. People think that as long as they were born again at one time, then they can live like hell and not have to ever worry about going there.

As with all Bible debates, it is a requirement to take both sides into account in order to find the complete true answer. Even though "sealed" and "irrevocable" and the other supporting scriptures can't mean "once saved, always saved," it is still necessary to explain what they do mean. Imagine if a man gave you a winning billion dollar lottery ticket. He tells you that all you have to do is to hold on to it for one month until the lottery association can get your money together. He tells you, "You have to be there and be ready to collect as soon as they tell you to or you won't get the money." As he gives this ticket to you, he promises you that "No person or no thing can ever take this ticket away from you. It's irrevocable." He says, "I have sealed this promise with you." You're so excited at first, but a couple of weeks later, you begin to doubt that the ticket is really a winner. You think to yourself, "This sounds too easy to be true." Your friends tell you that you're gullible and that you'll believe anything. Your doubt soon becomes total disbelief and anger. You never turned your ticket in because you didn't believe. Afterwards, you found out that the ticket really was a winner and that you never got to collect on your money because you weren't there and ready at the appointed time. You lost out on your big reward and you can never get it back now.

This is similar to how our salvation is. When we are born again, it's like we get a winning ticket. Instead of a billion dollars, this ticket is for eternal life with God and our saved loved ones. If you die having that ticket with you at the appointed time, then that means you've kept your faith and have done a reasonable job serving the Lord. However, if you die without that ticket, then somewhere down the line you've lost your faith in Christ, and you will not receive your gift of eternal life. This doesn't mean that God or anybody else took your salvation (or your ticket) away; it means that you never kept it till the end like Jesus told you to do (Matt. 10:22).

The purpose of this story is to understand how you can have something "sealed" and irrevocable" and yet, still lose it even though no one can take it from you. I'm certainly not trying to compare salvation with a lottery ticket. I'm only trying to show how the flexibility of the "once saved, always saved" supporting scriptures satisfies both sides of the supporting scriptures without compromising or ignoring any of the Bible. It won't work any other way. In a perfect world, this would hopefully be enough to at least get people thinking about whether or not their belief lines up with God's Word.

Clearly, Lucifer himself was in God's grace at one point in time since he was a most extraordinary angel (Ez. 28:12-14). God didn't just take the power and authority away from him for no reason. Lucifer gave it up when he decided to challenge the deity of God with his own divine ability. This is obviously an unacceptable sin, especially for someone in such a high position and trust (Is 14:12-14). This is another example of how everything we do comes with conditions and accountability.

In Romans 8:38-39, Paul tells us, *"For I am persuaded that neither death nor life, nor angels nor principalities nor powers, nor things present nor things to come, nor height nor depth, nor any other created thing, shall be able to separate us from the love of God which is in Christ Jesus our Lord."* This statement doesn't mean that everyone will love the Lord. It means that nothing can keep us from loving Him, and nothing will keep Him from loving us. God's Word is telling us that it is completely our own free will choice whether or not we have faith in Christ. If we don't, then we will inherit eternal death and hell. Not because God wants us to perish, but because we haven't accepted the one Way out of eternal hell that He provided for us. If we do believe, then there is nothing that can take our faith away from us except for ourself. This is what it means to have our salvation sealed with the Holy Spirit of promise until the day of our inheritance. And that will always be irrevocable.

II. What is the "age of accountability" and what about baptizing babies?

The age of accountability has always been a mystery for many Christians. It prompts the question, "At what age does someone have to be in order to be considered accountable for their belief in Christ?" Is it 6, 8, 12? What about autistic or mentally retarded people? Or what about the people stranded on a desert island that never get a chance to hear about Jesus? These are some very good questions that we can answer by using the Bible formula and some godly common sense.

a. Should we baptize infants?

Some Christians believe that everyone is accountable at birth and must be baptized with water as an infant, or they can't go to Heaven if they die. It's true that baptism is for the remission (forgiveness) of sins (Mark 1:4) and that we are all born into the original sin of Adam, but a water baptism will *never* remove that original sin. John the Baptist began baptizing people as a sign of repentance (Matt. 3:1). It would be impossible to repent from the original sin that you were born into since you have no control over it. Repentance really means to turn away from the sins that you've willingly committed. If we had to repent from the original sin that we were born into, then that means we would have to somehow leave our sinful bodies—not an option. The simple fact is that we will always be in our sinful bodies either until we die or until the Rapture. That is the reason why we must be born *again* by the Spirit. If a water baptism could remove the sin that we were born into, then we wouldn't have to wait until death or the Rapture to be physically rejoined with God again. We wouldn't need to be born again with the Holy Spirit. However, 2nd Corinthians 5:1–8 tells us that while we are in our earthly body "... *we are absent from the Lord.*" Verse 8 goes on to say that we can be confident knowing once we who are born again are absent from this body, we will be present with the Lord. If a water baptism could remove our original sin, then this statement would be false. It would then have to say, "Babies are absent from the Lord until they are baptized with water." An infant's only sin is the original sin they were born into. If water baptism removed this original sin, then there would be no *physical* separation between them and God. Knowing this, there would be no point, other than maybe a dedication to the Lord, to baptize infants or anyone who can't comprehend what it is. There certainly is no harm in baptizing babies, but it should be no substitute for being baptized as an accountable adult. Water baptisms in the Bible were all done only to older people that knew what they were doing and what it meant. Jesus was our supreme example.

We are told in Romans 10:9, *"that if you confess with our mouth the Lord Jesus and believe it in your heart that God has raised Him from the dead, you will be saved."* This is impossible for an infant that has no comprehension yet. Besides, God is not going to send a baby to hell for not being baptized because they're ignorant and unaccountable for their actions. We don't serve a murdering God who doesn't like to give us chances. We serve a just God who doesn't want any of us to perish (2nd Pet 3:9).

In Romans 5:13, Paul tells us, *"(For until the law sin was in the world, but sin is not imputed when there is no law)"* This means that even though everyone was born into the sin of Adam, we can't voluntarily sin against God unless we have laws to break in the first place. Jesus' sacrifice was sufficient for the sin we were born into as well as our sins by choice. If we have no sins from our own free will choices, then it's because we never received or we never got old or accountable enough to know God's laws. If this is the case, then Jesus' redemption for their sinful bodies (flesh) is all that is necessary for them to be rejoined with God. In the Old Testament days, even babies who died weren't able to go to Heaven until Jesus redeemed them of the original sin they were born into. They went to Paradise to wait with the other righteous saints who died. Now, since Christ has redeemed all of us, they can ascend directly to heaven. They need not ask for Jesus' forgiveness since they had no sin "*imputed.*"

One thing we can say for sure about babies and young children is that there is no limit on how early we can begin to serve God. We can start building up for our heavenly treasures as soon as we are able. Proverbs 20:11 tells us that, "*Even a child is known by his deeds, Whether what he does is pure and right.*"

b. At what point are we held accountable for accepting Christ?

If we go back to Adam and Eve in the Garden of Eden, we know they were created as adults. We know that they were ignorant to what was right and wrong *until* God gave them the choice to eat from the tree of knowledge of good and evil. Once they ate of that fruit, they immediately noticed their nakedness, and their eyes were open to what sin was. They knew that it was wrong to eat of that fruit, and they still did it. That made them accountable for their actions. We are accountable for our actions once we know the truth and still choose to do wrong. Only God knows for sure how much knowledge is enough to be held accountable. That is a gray area that we just don't have the right to say we know about for sure. However, this accountability is *not* limited to a certain age. It is solely determined by if and when you know right from wrong according what God's standards are. If someone was born mentally retarded, then that person will probably never eat of the fruit of knowledge of good and evil. People can only sin by choice if they disobey God's law. If they are incapable of knowing God's law, then God surely judges accordingly (Prov. 24:12). It's as if God, being just and fair, gives some people a free ticket to Heaven. They do still have to either die or be raptured in order to be rejoined with God since they were born into sin. But forgiveness and repentance is not possible for someone who has never had an opportunity to disobey God. So the next time you see mentally slow people being pushed in a wheelchair, know that God didn't curse them, He blessed them. Instead of feeling sorry for them, we need to be out reaching the ones who *do* know right from wrong yet are still choosing to do wrong. The same could be said for the death of a young child. A curse through worldly eyes could be a blessing through God's eyes.

For others who have never had an opportunity to hear about Jesus or about the way the Bible tells them to live, I believe the Book of Romans helps us to understand this. In Romans 2:14–15, Paul speaks of Gentiles (non-Jews who are ignorant to the law) who by nature do things according to God's law. He says that they will know right from wrong in their hearts and in their conscience. I guess an example of this could be if a tribe of people were living primitively on a remote island and never had an opportunity to hear about Jesus, then God (again being just and fair) will plant His laws in their hearts. To some degree, they should know right from wrong. They should know in their hearts that rape, theft, lying, murder, and so on are wrong and go against their conscience. According to the 2nd chapter of Romans, this is the way that God will judge some people. Proverbs 24:12 backs this up by stating that God takes into consideration our ignorance, and He will judge us accordingly. It says *"If you say, "Surely **we did not know** this," Does not He who weighs the hearts consider it? He who keeps your soul, does He not know it? And will He not render to each man according to his deeds?"* In this sense, there are still people who haven't heard the Gospel of Christ that will be judged and ultimately saved by the law that God puts in their hearts. Yes, Paul says in Romans 7:6 that, *"... we have been delivered from the law..."* but this is referring to the people who have heard about the Gospel of Jesus. Romans 7:4 states that *"... you have also become dead to the law **through** the body of Christ..."* If you've never heard of Jesus and have not had the opportunity to be in the Body of Christ, then the law still applies to you for salvation.

This covenant that God has with the ignorant people who don't know the Bible is similar to the covenant that the Old Testament saints were under. In both instances, salvation comes through the law because they haven't been fortunate enough to hear about Christ. It doesn't negate the fact that we can only come to the Father through the Son, Jesus. If it hadn't been for Jesus redeeming mankind of our sins, then even the ignorant people who hadn't heard of Him couldn't receive salvation, whether it was through God's law or by faith in Christ. Any way you look at it, salvation can only come through the cross.

It is our responsibility as Christians to make people accountable for making a decision for Christ. We do this by sharing the Good News of the Gospel with them. If we plant this Good News in someone's heart, then the Holy Spirit can convict them if they choose not to serve Him. Only God knows exactly how much information is sufficient for someone to be considered accountable. Every day, more and more of the world is hearing about Christ. This is good news for those of us who believe, but it's not so good for the ones who won't accept Christ. For example, most of the people in a Christian nation like the Unites States have certainly heard the Truth about Jesus. Now we are accountable for our actions because of that. Ignorance will not be an excuse for the Americans who reject Christ, as long as we are capable of knowing right from wrong. It is such a blessing to live in a time when we can openly serve Jesus, but on the other hand, there is a lot more accountability for such a nation. The Bible tells us in Luke 12:48, "... *For everyone to whom much is given, from him much will be required* ..." This is why the church needs to strengthen up and reclaim our Christian foundation. We as believers can start by targeting the enemy of this world instead of other Christians.

c. At what point were the Jews accountable for accepting Christ?

In the first century A.D., the Gospel of Christ was being spread throughout the world, but at first, not all of the Jews had a chance to hear about Jesus. Does this mean that after the Day of Pentecost, the Jews who lived and died under the old covenant and hadn't yet heard of the new covenant went to hell? Was there a certain day when the new covenant kicked in for everyone whether they heard about Jesus or not? God's Word tells us the answer to these questions in Hebrews 10. Here, the author's purpose was to lead Jews to Jesus by explaining how Christ fulfilled the old Law. In Hebrews 10:26, the Jews were warned that, "... *if we sin willfully after we have received the knowledge of the truth, there no longer remains a sacrifice for our sins* ..." If we break this verse down into segments, then we can understand it better. For the Jews to "sin willfully" after they know the "truth" clearly means that they are accountable for these actions. This is not referring to original sin. The "truth" is Jesus Christ. In John 14:6, Jesus tells us, "... *I am the way, the **truth**, and the life* ..." Under the old law, sins were covered up by different sacrifices. What God's Word is telling us is that if we willfully commit sins after we have heard the "truth" about Jesus, then sacrifices will not remove your sins anymore like they did under the Law of Moses. Only the blood of Jesus that was shed on Calvary can forgive these sins.

If we use this Scripture in its proper context, then we can see that the Jews who did accept Jesus as the Son of God went into a transition period between the old and new covenant. The Jews were not accountable to be under the new covenant until they received knowledge of it. But once they heard enough of the Good News to make them accountable, then they could no longer be saved by the old Law, whether they accepted Jesus or not. The job of the early disciples was to convert Jews and Gentiles to Christianity by spreading the Gospel of Jesus. That commission must continue through us as the disciples of this age. Ezekiel was warned by God to tell the lost sinners about Him and His conditions, or else their blood would be on his (Ezekiel's) hands. I believe there are people in our lives that we are responsible for making accountable by telling them about Jesus as well. I'm sure we all know someone whose only chance of hearing the Gospel is whether or not we decide to share it with them. What a horrible feeling it will be to one day see all the ones who we had a chance to reach but never took the time.

8 Putting It All Together

Part 2 The Power of the Holy Spirit

We've gone through a couple of doctrines by using the information and guidelines that have been laid out so far in this book. Since practice makes perfect, I think it would be helpful to search out and study a couple more very important church-dividing doctrines. Not only will you be able to solve Bible mysteries better, but you will hopefully dig deeper into some new truths along the way.

I. What does it mean to be "baptized with the Holy Spirit"?

The first subject we are going to look at in this chapter is the baptism with the Holy Spirit. This has been the subject of many different interpretations. By hearing many of these different views on this subject, it has helped me to put them all together and come up with the one and only answer that I believe lines up with *all* of God's Word.

Let's start by reading a quote from John the Baptist in Luke 3:16, where it says, *"John answered, saying to all, 'I indeed baptize you with water; but One mightier than I is coming, whose sandal strap I am not worthy to loose. He will baptize you with the Holy Spirit and fire.'"* As we see a couple of more verses into this chapter, John is referring to Jesus, the promised Messiah, who will come and baptize with the Holy Spirit. There are two important truths that we should identify from this passage. First, no one has ever been baptized with the Holy Spirit and with fire up to this point in history. Second, Jesus Christ is the only one who can baptize people with the Holy Spirit. John was telling the people that he could baptize with water, but only Jesus could baptize with the Spirit. As we'll see later, this special Spirit baptism is the consummation of God's plan of salvation.

It's important not to confuse the "baptism with the Holy Spirit" with being "filled with the Holy Spirit." The word "baptism" means to be submerged or buried. In Colossians 2:12, Paul says that we are ***buried with Him in baptism . . .*** " We can be submerged with the Spirit without necessarily being filled. For example, let's say you took an empty Mason jar that was sealed and dunked it into a tub of water. It would be submerged (or baptized) in the water, but it wouldn't be filled unless you opened the lid and let the water pour into it. Being submerged and being filled are two totally separate events. That doesn't mean they can't happen simultaneously. The Mason jar could certainly be submerged and filled at the same time if the lid was off. It just means they're not the same experience. I will explain what it is to be filled with the Spirit later in this chapter. For now, we're going to look at the baptism with the Holy Spirit.

I said before that it is the Holy Spirit who will one day take your soul to heaven. Without Him, you have no way to get there. We already know you will need to be born again (or born of Spirit) to receive this Holy Spirit (John 3:5). This "born again" experience of accepting Christ into your heart is what I believe the Bible refers to as being "baptized with the Holy Spirit." There is not any one Scripture to prove this belief, but if we use many scriptures combined, then I think you'll see that this is true.

The first reason why I believe this special Spirit baptism is the same as converting to Christ is because of the meaning of the word "baptism." In the same illustration used earlier, let's put ourselves in place of the Mason jar and replace the tub of water with the Holy Spirit. When we accept Jesus as our Lord and Savior, it's like Jesus submerges (or baptizes) us with His Spirit. Now unless we walk away from our faith in Christ, we have the Holy Spirit around us to take our souls to Heaven and be reunited with our original Creator. Since the word "baptized" means "to be surrounded by," then we should see it as an external experience and not the same as an internal filling.

The second reason for this belief is because the disciples had the Holy Spirit given to them by Jesus (which was the Spirit baptism), but it wasn't until a few days later that they were filled or empowered with the Spirit. We can prove this by combining a few scriptures together. We know from John 20:22 that *before* the Day of Pentecost, Jesus breathed on the disciples and then they did "*... Receive the Holy Spirit."* We know from reading Luke 24:49 that Jesus referred to this particular Holy Spirit experience as the "*... Promise of My Father..."* In Acts 1:4–5, Jesus comes right out and tells us that the "Promise of the Father" *is* the baptism with the Holy Spirit. Now if we look at Luke 24:49 with what we know from Jesus' own words, it could read like this (helps added in bold): "*Behold, I send the **Promise of My Father** upon you* (Behold, I baptize you with the Holy Spirit); *but tarry in the city of Jerusalem until you are endued with power from on high.* (but wait in Jerusalem until you are filled with the Spirit and endued with power)" This not only shows us that the baptism with the Holy Spirit is the same as our born again conversion, but it also shows us that this is a different experience than being filled with the Holy Spirit. To reassure that the "Promise of the Father" is the same as "receiving the Holy Spirit" as the disciples did (John 20:22), look at what Peter say's in Acts 2:38–39: "*... Repent, and... be baptized in the name of Jesus Christ... and you shall **receive** the gift of the Holy Spirit. For the **promise** is to you, to your children and to all ..."* By searching out different scriptures, we can see in Jesus' own words as well as others what it means to be baptized with the Spirit. Having said that, we can conclude that when Jesus told the apostles in Acts 1:4 to wait for the "Promise of the Father," He must have been referring to everyone else receiving this Promise. Jesus was saying this Promise would soon be available to everybody and that He didn't want the apostles to leave before it came. There were certainly enough people in the upper room who didn't have the Holy Spirit yet that Jesus could have been referring to. It wouldn't make sense for Jesus to tell the disciples to wait for something that He already gave them. This is where you have to identify flexible scriptures and make sure that all pertaining scriptures are satisfied. If the disciples had not yet been baptized with the Holy Spirit, then John 20:22 and Luke 24:49 would be incorrect.

The third reason that I believe the baptism with the Holy Spirit is the same as being born again is because of the time line. We don't read about this event taking place in the Bible until the Day of Pentecost (Acts 2), fifty days after the resurrection of Jesus. It's more than a coincidence that this is the same day that salvation through the new covenant was made available to every person in the world (Acts 2:21). If the Day of Pentecost was the first opportunity for believers to be born again of the Holy Spirit (except for Jesus' disciples, who already personally received the Holy Ghost in John 20:22), then don't you think there would be a bigger fuss made about eternal life than about speaking in tongues or other empowering spiritual gifts? Clearly, it was eternal life through Christ that was the main subject here. Endowment of power from on high is an added bonus for us to better spread the Gospel (Acts 1:8). The baptism with the Holy Spirit was not available until Jesus fulfilled His earthly sacrifice. John 7:39 tells us before this time "... *the Holy Spirit was **not yet given**, because Jesus was not yet glorified.*" Again, it's more than a coincidence that the same day the baptism with the Holy Spirit was given was the same day that salvation was made possible for everyone through Jesus. Surely they're both one in the same experience.

The last reason why I believe the Spirit baptism is the same as being Spirit born is because of what the Apostle Paul wrote in 1st Corinthians 12:13. Here, we read, "*For by one **Spirit** we were **all baptized** into one body . . .*" If the baptism with the Spirit meant speaking in tongues or anything other than conversion into the body of Christ, then this Scripture would be inaccurate. Only some would be baptized into one body if that were the case.

A challenge surrounding this issue is discerning what the New Testament authors always meant when they use phrases such as "and they received the Holy Spirit," or "the Holy Spirit fell upon them," and so on. I pray that you can see through the examples in this book how to use the Bible to find the answers to these phrases as well as other doctrines that are difficult to discern. The one thing to remember is that the real answer should line up with every Scripture that pertains to that belief.

II. What does it mean to be "filled with the holy spirit"?

The next questions that we're going to try to resolve by using the Bible formula is: What exactly does it mean to be filled with the Holy Spirit? Many Christians debate over what this awesome experience really is. Some people call it the "baptism with the Holy Ghost." I just listed several reasons why that's not logical. Some call it "filled with the Holy Ghost," and some just call it "endued with power from on high." For the sake of argument, I'll just call this experience being "filled with the Holy Ghost."

Many churches are divided as to what happens when God initially fills someone with the Holy Spirit. Like we read in chapter 4 of this book, some churches don't even believe that spiritual gifts and endowment of God's power are for today. However, there is nothing in God's Word that should make us believe this divine power was just used to get the church started. This is a false teaching that many people add to the Bible. This should not even be a church dividing factor.

I'm going to stress again that being "born again" doesn't necessarily mean that you're filled with the Holy Ghost, even though you can receive your salvation and be filled with the Holy Ghost at the same time (Acts 19:5–6). Being filled is when you receive an endowment of God's power for the sake of leading souls to Christ. It's not a "level" of Christianity that allows you to just stop seeking the Lord once you've been filled. In fact, we have to strive to remain filled with the Holy Spirit as often as we can. It's like filling your car with gas so that it won't run out and quit working. Paul tells us in Ephesians 5:18, *"And do not be drunk with wine, in which is dissipation; but be **filled** with the Spirit."* Paul is telling us not to be like the drunkard that stays filled on wine constantly, but to constantly fill ourselves with the Holy Spirit. There were many times in the Bible that Peter and Paul were filled on different occasions for certain circumstances.

a. Is being filled with the Holy Ghost the same in the Old Testament as it is in the New Testament?

Absolutely! The only experience that is new under our covenant is being born again or "baptized" with the Holy Spirit. A person being empowered by God is not a new experience. Notice in the first chapter of Luke that John the Baptist was *filled "... with the Holy Spirit, even from his mother's womb."* (Luke 1:15). Compare this with the fact that Jesus was *conceived by* the Holy Spirit (Luke 1:35). These are two completely different experiences. Jesus was the first human to be born by the Holy Spirit in this manner. He set the example for all of us to follow. After Jesus' death and resurrection, this birth was a means for eternal life. However, being filled with the Holy Spirit was God's way of supplying His people with power to further His kingdom.

The endowment of supernatural power from God has always been around. Peter and everyone with him on the Day of Pentecost certainly were not the first people to be filled with the Holy Spirit. The Bible lists several people under the old covenant who were given supernatural power by being filled with the Spirit. Besides John the Baptist, there were Bezalel (Ex. 31:1–3, Ex. 35:31), Elizabeth (Luke 1:41), Zacharias (Luke 1:67), and many more. In fact, every true prophet of God could not prophesy unless they were filled with the Spirit of God (2nd Pet. 1:21). One of the two Hebrew words for *prophet* is nabi,' which means "to bubble forth." Imagine God filling you up with His Spirit until it bubbles over onto someone else. This overflow is the supernatural power that God will use for His glory. It could be speaking in other tongues, prophesying, healing, overwhelming joy, wisdom, boldness to preach the Word of God, or anything else that God wills. Whatever the case may be, you or the person(s) around you will be edified for the glory of God.

There is no difference in the *quality* of this power from God between the old and new covenant. However, there is a difference in the *quantity*. Before the Day of Pentecost, God chose the people in which He empowered with certain spiritual gifts. The Bible tells us that in Samuel's day (about 1150 B.C.), "*...And the word of the Lord was rare in those days; there was no widespread revelation.*" (1st

Sam. 3:1). Since the Day of Pentecost, however, God has offered this empowerment to anyone who calls on the name of the Lord (Acts 2:17–21). You and I have every right to this empowerment, and we can pray and seek after the spiritual gifts that we desire. But ultimately, it is God who decides which gifts we do and do not get.

b. Is tongues the only evidence of being filled with the Holy Spirit?

The Bible defines the experience of being filled with the Holy Spirit as an endowment of supernatural power from on high that enables you to become an effective witness for Jesus Christ. Acts 1:8 tells us, *"But you shall receive **power** when the Holy Spirit has come upon you; and you shall be **witnesses** to me in Jerusalem, and in all Judea and Samaria, and to the ends of the earth."* It's worth repeating that being a powerful witness for Him in a way that you could never have been before is the *one and only* guaranteed evidence that you've been filled with God's Spirit.

This supernatural power could be manifested several different ways. Paul lists several different gifts of the Holy Spirit such as faith, healing, prophesy, speaking and interpreting other tongues, and more. In Acts, Luke writes about other evidences of being filled like boldness and the ability to preach about Jesus. Being filled with the Holy Spirit is like pouring water into a glass. Instead of stopping when you've reached the top of the glass, you just keep pouring so that the water keeps spilling over. When God fills us with His Spirit, then there will also be an overspill. This Spirit overspill is what God used to edify others to help build His kingdom. I mentioned earlier that in Acts 5:15–16, Peter was so filled up with the Spirit that when his shadow passed over the sick people that were lying in the streets, they were all healed. Again, notice the difference between being surrounded and being filled with the Holy Spirit. The same Spirit could overfill you with joy, faith, love, the gift of miracles, the interpreting and speaking of tongues, boldness, wisdom, leadership skills, and so much more. The important thing to remember is that God knows what gifts we need to do the job that we are called to do. I'm convinced that this was Paul's message in 1st Corinthians 12:31 when he said to "... *earnestly desire the **best** gifts* ..." We need to desire and pray for the "best gifts" that suit our calling.

A huge misconception in many churches is that when God fills you with the Holy Spirit, then you *must* initially speak in tongues. They believe this is the evidence that God gives us every time so that we can be sure we're filled. I believe the Bible tells us something different if we just take the time to use *all* of the pertaining scriptures.

c. What is the gift of tongues?

If we study the scriptures that explain what spiritual gifts are (especially the gift of tongues), then the Bible can solve this debate for us. In 1st Corinthians 12:4–11, Paul explains that there are different gifts and manifestations of the Spirit that are given to each person in order to profit everybody. Paul then lists nine examples of gifts we could receive in order to effectively do our ministry for Jesus. Notice in 1st Corinthians 12:10, Paul lists one of the Spiritual gifts as "... *different kinds of tongues* ..." In every case, the gift of tongues is a language that is unknown to the person who is speaking it. Through the utterance of the Holy Spirit, those who have this gift can speak this unlearned language. "Different kinds of tongues" doesn't just mean different languages; it means different *kinds* of languages. Paul tells us about only two separate *kinds* of tongues in 1st Corinthians 13:1. There are "... *tongues of **men** and of **angels*** ..." Therefore, both kinds must be included in this list. This means that these two kinds of tongues may or may not be a gift that God wills for us all to have. God wants us each to have the best gifts that fit the calling of our life. These two kinds of tongues are just two of the many ways to build up God's kingdom, but it's not the only way. Many times in the Bible it is hard to tell which of these kinds of tongues is being referred to because of the two thousand year culture difference between then and now. I would imagine that in Peter and Paul's day, it would have been a lot clearer to understand than it is now looking back. Even though it's hard to always tell, the Bible does give us direction as to the different manifestations of these gifts of tongues.

The first kind of tongue is the "tongues of men," which is a gift from God that can be used in two different ways. One way is for the edification of a church body, but *only when it is interpreted*. This is one way that God will bring a message to the church. 1st Corinthians 14:10–13 explains this tongue as a foreign language that should be interpreted for the edification of the whole church. When this kind of tongue is interpreted by revelation (which is another spiritual gift), then it's as effective for the church as prophesying is (1st Cor. 14:5). If there is no one to interpret, then there should be no message brought in tongues (1st Cor. 14:28).

The second way that the "tongues of men" can be used is as sign to an unbeliever (1st Cor. 14:22). Again, this is when you will speak a language that is totally unknown to you, but there will be one or more unbelievers around you who do speak that language and understand it perfectly. This will be a sign to them because not only did you speak an unknown language, but you also gave the foreigner(s) a message from God in their own language. This is the kind of tongue that was used mightily on the Day of Pentecost (Acts 2:4–11).

The other kind of tongue is the tongues of angels. The tongues of angels are also called a prayer language or a devotional tongue. This is a gift that allows the believer, as he is filled with the Spirit, to speak to God in a language that *only* God can understand (1st Cor. 14:2). It is essentially our spirit praying for us when we don't know how or what to pray (1st Cor. 14:14). Many churches (at least the ones who believe in spiritual gifts) teach that this "prayer language" is given to everyone who gets filled (or as they call it—baptized) with the Holy Ghost as the initial evidence. This belief contradicts the definition of endowment of power that Acts 1:8 gives us. We already know that this passage tells us that this empowerment of God's Spirit will make us a supernatural witness for Jesus. Speaking in this prayer language or angelic tongue is only understood by God, so it can't be too effective for witnessing. In 1st Cor. 14:19, Paul refers to this particular tongue when he says, "*…yet in the church I would rather speak five words with my understanding, that I may teach others also, than ten thousand words in a tongue.*" I'm not saying that this gift has no part in witnessing, and neither was Paul. I just believe there are other, better gifts to focus our prayers on instead of "overshooting" this one.

Another problem with the "tongues only" belief is that is if we study 1st Corinthians 12 in its entire context, we can see Paul stressing the point about why different people need different gifts. He says in verse 17, *"If the whole body were an eye, then where would be the hearing? If the whole were hearing, where would be the smelling?"* In verses 29–31, Paul clearly says that not everyone will speak in tongues, or heal, or teach, etc., but that we should seek the spiritual gifts that suit our calling. This is the reason that in 1st Corinthians 12:11, we read that God distributes each gift according to *His* will for our lives, not our will. This means that we can't make ourselves speak in tongues or prophesy or be a pastor if it's not God's will for us. However, if we excel in our own calling and not someone else's calling, then the entire church would profit (1st Cor. 12:7).

Ironically, many of the churches that teach of this angelic tongue (or prayer language) as being the initial evidence of being filled with the Holy Ghost use the Day of Pentecost as their Scripture base because of the one hundred twenty people who spoke in tongues as the Spirit gave them utterance (Acts 2:4). The problem with this is that on that day, they didn't speak in that angelic prayer language that can only be understood by God (1st Cor. 14:2). They spoke in languages that the foreign people outside could hear and understand because it was their own language. This was a sign to them that the Holy Spirit had fully come just like Joel predicted He would (Acts 2:16–21). So if the initial response to being Spirit filled is always speaking in tongues, then shouldn't there always be some people around who understand the tongue that you're speaking? After all, that's what happened on the Day of Pentecost (Acts 2). It would be more believable for God to distribute this kind of tongue once we get filled with the Spirit than the angelic tongue. If we were to assume that the initial evidence of being filled with the Spirit is speaking in an angelic tongue, then listen to what we would have to assume about the one hundred twenty people in the upper room on the Day of Pentecost: We would have to assume that they all initially started speaking in tongues that only God could understand. Then somewhere after that their language must have switched over to foreign tongues that only the people around them could understand.

This is an awfully big assumption, especially since the Bible doesn't even begin to tell us that this is how it happened. We know that God is not an author of confusion, so it's important that we do not add anything to His Word to form our own doctrines. This is also another reason why we can't build a belief or even a church on one particular Bible verse. We have to look at the whole picture to find the whole truth.

In the Bible, we can read about people getting filled with the Holy Ghost and *not* initially speaking in tongues. Starting in Acts 4:29, Peter and John prayed that the believers, even though they were forbidden to preach the Gospel of Christ, would boldly speak God's Word. Verse 31 says "*... they were all filled with the Holy Spirit, and they spoke the word of God with boldness.*" Boldness was the supernatural power that they really needed at this point in time. Speaking in tongues would not have been the most effective gift in that circumstance. So in that case, it was God's will that they received boldness. Another example in the Bible is in Acts 9:17–20, when the apostle Paul (called Saul at that time) got filled with the Holy Ghost for the first time. His immediate reaction to being filled wasn't to speak in tongues, but instead he preached the Christ in the synagogues. This was a complete heart change for this same man who once destroyed people for calling on the name of Jesus (Acts 9:21). We know that sometime later Paul did receive the gift of speaking in tongues (1st Cor. 13:1), but his initial "evidence" of being filled with the Holy Spirit was that he preached that Christ is the Son of God.

After looking at all of these pertaining scriptures, we can come to this conclusion: Although the gift of tongues is for today, it's not the only gift that we should focus on as the evidence of being filled with the Holy Spirit. This subject is a huge church-divider, so we really need to put on our unbiased thinking cap in order to find the truth. Stubbornness will only keep you where the devil wants you—fighting other Christians. 1st Samuel 15:23 gives us a firm warning of this when he says, "*... stubbornness is as iniquity and **idolatry**, Because you have rejected the word of the Lord ...*" This is because when we ignore the Word of God about a certain doctrine because it's not the explanation we want, then we have made ourselves like idols being exalted above God and His Word.

I can't say for sure what everyone's Spirit filling experience will be like. I can tell you that it will be an experience you will never forget. It will be one that keeps you coming back for more.

I have only touched on a few of the debated subjects that have divided churches into denominations. It is my prayer that you've learned how to discern these debates by using the Bible and by having an open mind to the truth. Now take this training and establish more faith in what you believe in by letting God's Word show you. Being a dedicated servant to the Lord shouldn't be about you and me. It should be all about Jesus and what we can do to better serve Him by following His Word. Know that there's only one right answer—God's answer. It's up to us to try to find it. God's Word is alive, and it can reveal things to you that you could never see on your own. All we have to do is put forth the effort.

9 The Conclusion

I hope this book can be used as a guide to further your faith in Christ. I also hope you've seen the importance of an undivided church body. Of course, that doesn't mean every Christian will always agree with one another, but we shouldn't let doctrines split us up, especially the ones that are easy to understand by using all the scriptures that are attributed to them. None of us will ever have all the answers. However, I do believe you can find the answers to most of your toughest questions by using the methods described in this book. It is God's will for us to know His mysteries and to "*... always be ready to give a defense to everyone who asks you a reason for the hope that is in you...*" (1st Peter 3:15).

I. Review

As a review, let's look at some powerful ways to understand the Bible the way God wanted us to. Once you have seen and understood God's plan of salvation from beginning to end, then the rest will line up much easier. You should begin by praying and asking God for His guidance. He has great pleasure in us when we search out the truth, and He wants to help us in every way. That's why He gave us the Holy Spirit to help us understand. You don't have to be a genius to study the Bible. God will use anybody who is willing, especially when the odds are not in our favor. This is when He is glorified the most. Many times in the Bible, God reduced the odds so that when there was victory, then He got all of the credit (Judges 7). Keep your eyes on Him, and keep your faith in Him so you can be used mightily and not get discouraged about your ability. God is bigger than any man-made obstacle that tries to get in our way. God gave me instruction to write this book, so I wrote it. I can't worry about questions like, "Who will want to read it?" or "How will a nobody like me ever get it published?" The God I serve is all-powerful, and He can do anything He wants.

It's important not to overshoot anything in the Bible, but to read it as God intended. It's equally as important not to understate a subject in the Bible just to balance out someone else's exaggeration of it. The point here is that we accept everything in the Bible the way God wanted it to be, and not any more or any less. Make sure every reference you ever use in the Bible is not taken out of context. If you're not sure, then read a chapter before and a chapter after to help. Reference Bibles can help you find other places that talk about the same subject also. Ask your spiritual advisors for their help.

Always remember that there are no contradictions in the Bible. If there appears to be one, then you have to plug every related verse into the Bible formula in order to get the truth. Don't be discouraged if you don't find the answer to certain questions right away. It took over a year for God to finally reveal to me some of the doctrines explained in this book. One last time, if you're struggling with a certain Bible doctrine and you're not sure what to believe, then there are several things you can do. First, make sure you're asking God for His guidance at all times. Make sure you're heart is right with Him so your line of communication isn't clogged with sin. Second, make sure your motive is pure for finding these Biblical truths. If you just want to prove someone else wrong, then don't expect God's help. Third, find all of the scriptures that pertain to that subject. This may require some help from many diverse people with different opinions. Fourth, study each doctrine in the proper context of the book in which it was written. Finally, identify which scriptures have the potential to flex and which ones don't. Once you've done all of these things, then find the answer that supports *all* of those scriptures. Hopefully, you will come up with a better idea of what you should believe in.

Always be sure to pray first and be opened-minded. If you're not prepared to change your beliefs for any reason, then you would be wasting your time doing this in the first place. If someone disagrees with you on a particular belief and he shows you Bible Scripture to back his belief up, don't just give him your side of the debate. Look up his side for yourself to see if you have to go back to the drawing board. Use his scriptures to figure out if you missed something on this subject. Plug his scriptures in with yours and see if maybe you're either wrong or at least incomplete in this belief. You might both be wrong. Maybe by combining the whole truth you'll see something new that satisfies all related Bible verses. Again, if there are any scriptures that are used properly and still disagree with a belief you have, then keep on searching. There has to be an answer that satisfies the whole Bible.

II. How can we make a difference?

Too often, people think that if they can't make a *big* difference, then it's not worth trying. This is the same reason why many people don't vote in presidential elections. The truth is that we can't always make a big impact on the world. God never expected us to. However, we can do our part as an individual member of one whole body. Satan has had so much success with this country and the world by taking small steps each time. He has also been successful by dividing the churches into denominations and smaller groups because he knows that they are easier to manipulate than a large, unified team. We need to understand that if we're going to have any type of Christian revival today, then it's not going to happen overnight. Individually, we can't do a whole lot, but as a whole, we can make a difference. Unity is the first step. If we can start by uniting, then we can look to the next obstacle and go from there. It's easy to get discouraged and think you can't help this lost world when you look at the news and see what's going on. I would advise you not to worry about those things that you have no control over, but concentrate in the areas where you can be used by God. Start with your family, your friends, your co-workers, your neighbors, your church, and most importantly, yourself.

If you have used this Bible formula and you have established a belief that your church disagrees with, pull your pastors or teachers aside and show them what you found. Maybe they will show you some scriptures that you missed. Maybe they will tell you to get lost. It's my prayer that if you are right according to the Bible and they're wrong, then they would change their belief on that particular subject. If they refuse to change their views without giving you a logical reason for not doing so, then you can assume that they are set in their ways and are too stubborn to be reproved by God's Word. In this circumstance, I would say to keep that church in constant prayer (which you should do anyway). If it continues, find a church another church with a leader who *will* submit to God's Word. It's more important to submit to the Bible than to always have to be right. If scriptural correction is brought to you through someone else, then you shouldn't think of it as though that *person* corrected you. You should see it as God's Word that corrected you. Since this is the case, then it shouldn't matter who brings correction from the Bible to you, even if it's a child. In fact, you should want people who will tell you when something isn't right as long as they do it in love and not out of pride. One of my favorite scriptures in the Bible is Proverbs 12:1. It says, "*Whoever loves instruction loves knowledge, but he who hates correction is stupid.*" God made us all to be used together as one team (or body). We each have our own strengths and weaknesses, so why not lean on each other?

III. How can the church leaders make a difference?

To the pastors, teachers, evangelists, priests, prophets, music leaders and whoever else: I beg you to search out the beliefs of your church and make sure that they're God's commands, not man's traditions. In order for some churches to completely line up with God's Word, they may need to go against the doctrine of their denomination. It may even mean losing your position for what you believe in. If this is the case, then remember that you are called by God and not by man. Your calling goes with you (this is the true meaning of irrevocable). God will certainly not condemn you for trying to break down the divisions of His church and bringing unity back into the spotlight. A problem in many churches is that there is little or no freedom to change your views on certain subjects because of the covering (or umbrella) that the church is under. In order for us to learn, we have to always remain teachable. If we assume that our beliefs and our church's doctrines are perfect, then we have put restrictions on the Holy Spirit. We are no longer teachable. The apostle Paul stresses the point of a non-divisional church (1st Cor. 1:10). This is a church without labels. It's a church where everyone tries to look at everyone else's good qualities instead of the bad ones. Christians are not judged for their appearance, spiritual gifts, financial status, sex, race, or anything else. If someone needs to be shown that they're in sin, then it's our job to care about them enough to help them *as long as our motive is love*!

Another mistake that must be avoided is putting a "non-denominational" name tag on a very denominational church. This is a deceptive trick that might fool church members, but it won't fool God. Stand up for the truth, remembering that Romans 8:31 tells us, "... *If God is for us, who can be against us?*" This is where you can make the biggest impact. By saying "no" to repetitious religion and "yes" to the Bible, you can have many more churches and believers in general teaming up with you. Instead of pointing out your differences, you can fight on the same team against the real enemy. This is a church with power from on high.

I thank you for taking the time to read this. I hope it can be used as a reference guide along side of the greatest book ever written—the Holy Bible. I love you all, and I can't wait to share our experiences together in Heaven.

TATE PUBLISHING & *Enterprises*

Tate Publishing is committed to excellence in the publishing industry. Our staff of highly trained professionals, including editors, graphic designers, and marketing personnel, work together to produce the very finest books available. The company reflects the philosophy established by the founders, based on Psalms 68:11,

"THE LORD GAVE THE WORD AND GREAT WAS THE COMPANY OF THOSE WHO PUBLISHED IT."

If you would like further information, please call 1.888.361.9473
or visit our website
www.tatepublishing.com

TATE PUBLISHING & *Enterprises*, LLC
127 E. Trade Center Terrace
Mustang, Oklahoma 73064 USA